Unbelievably Good Deals That You Absolutely Can't Get Unless You're a Teacher

SECOND EDITION

BARRY HARRINGTON and BETH CHRISTENSEN

CB
CONTEMPORARY BOOKS

Library of Congress Cataloging-in-Publication Data

Harrington, Barry.
    Unbelievably good deals that you absolutely can't get unless you're a
teacher / Barry Harrington and Beth Christensen. — 2nd ed.
      p.   cm.
    Includes index.
    ISBN 0-8092-2877-7
      1. Teaching—Aids and devices—Directories.   2. Audio-visual
material—United States—Directories.   3. Free material—United States—
Directories.   4. Publishers—United States—Directories.   5.
Corporations—United States—Directories.   6. Associations, institutions,
etc.—United States—Directories.   I. Christensen, Beth.   II. Title.
LB1044.88.H37   1995
371.33'025—dc21   98-33512
                                            CIP

The information in this book is up to date at the time of publication. Shipping and
handling charges and other facts are subject to change.

Cover design by Kim Bartko

Published by Contemporary Books
A division of NTC/Contemporary Publishing Group, Inc.
4255 West Touhy Avenue, Lincolnwood (Chicago), Illinois 60646-1975 U.S.A.
Printed in the United States of America
International Standard Book Number: 0-8092-2877-7
17   16   15   14   13   12   11   10   9   8   7   6   5   4   3   2   1

This book is dedicated to the memory of
Kris Hillebrand.

And also to my father, Thomas H. Harrington
(1930–1996), a man of foresight and genius whose
pioneering work in recycling and alternative energy
renders his untimely passing a loss not only to our
family but to the world.

—BH

Contents

Preface

In Ray Bradbury's short story "The Toynbee Convector," a time traveler journeys one hundred years into the future and comes back with a message of hope for the world.

In the future, the time traveler says, mankind does not destroy the world. Instead, we rebuild it; we fix the inner cities and small towns alike. We clean the rivers and stop war, cancer, and death. Upon hearing this good news, the people cry with joy and run to build that future. In Bradbury's tale, the twist is that the time traveler never went to the future at all; his "inspired fraudulence" was ultimately a way to offer civilization vision and hope. In one shot, the mythical traveler undid the bad fruits of the 20th century's nihilism and unshackled society from its conditioning and negative thinking. The story inspires because of its possibilities.

The power and strength to change frequently comes, oddly enough, in life's darkest moments—when schools are fraught with disaster, for example, or when AIDS plagues a generation, riots erupt in our cities, and drugs and gangs kill our youth.

We live in both an incredibly good—and an incredibly bad—era. We have established a society that is both extremely advanced and remarkably shortsighted, both civilized and brutal, both tolerant and unjust. If we agree where the problems are—or at least agree that our nation (and global village) needs to deal with serious issues—we begin to wake from our national nightmare.

And what single function in society intersects our memories of the past, our current skills, and our dreams for the future? Education, of course. Used powerfully and reshaped appropriately, education can act as a magnet, drawing together communities and civilization into a bright 21st century. The technological revolution is already upon us. We merely need to heed the call of globalization and see that problem solving is often best done by simply making connections—between educators and businesspeople, between ideas and actions.

A fundamental sense of optimism has always been at the root of the American subconscious. (The very fact that you chose the challenging profession of teaching suggests you possess an optimistic nature.) But that sense of optimism, once declared a birthright, has now been lost, perhaps even stolen from the kids of today—maybe because society has overlooked them for too long. It is this sense of helplessness that is being expressed by "Generation X," when it explains why even *trying* in the current system feels futile.

Eknath Easwaran, the transplanted Indian mystic and former Fulbright visiting scholar at the University of California at Berkeley, expresses the terrible truth in his book *Original Goodness*:

> The president of the American Association of Suicidology estimated . . . that half a million of our teenagers attempt suicide each year. In a free and affluent society such as ours, why would so many of our children come to the conclusion that their lives are not worth pursuing? It is tempting to point a finger at specific causes like drugs, but the president of the Youth Suicide National Center in Washington looks deeper. Our young people are profoundly troubled, she says, because "their sense of future is gone."
>
> Global threats like environmental disaster and nuclear war are enough to undermine anyone's sense of future. Yet even more damaging, in my opinion, is the lack of a sustaining purpose. With a higher goal, human beings can face any challenge. But without a goal, the spirit withers, and when the natural idealism of the young is blocked, their energy eventually breaks through into uncontrolled and often self-destructive channels. Most young people I know do not really want an easy life. They look for challenge: real challenges, all the bigger because their capacities are so huge. All they ask is something to live for. But we have become a culture without large goals, with nothing but material abundance to offer the hunger in their hearts.

It becomes clear that we, as a society, must do "something"

to solve the problems all around us and make the world a more habitable, operative place.

How?

First of all, by refusing to be intimidated by such lofty and impossible-sounding goals as "society working together to change the world." Society, after all, is us . . . you, me, the street youth who sells drugs because it is the "best" way to make money, and your neighbor who thinks corporation heads and environmentalists can never get along.

Second, by supporting in any way possible America's teachers, the portion of society that links our nation's children and the future. During a good part of every weekday, the very lives and well-being of children are out of the hands of parents and in the hands of teachers. Moreover, the duties of not only conveying instructional material but also of coping with basic security issues and developing students' self-esteem all too often fall to teachers.

In the face of the basic material shortfalls prevalent in the national education system, teachers often find themselves spending personal funds to enhance their classrooms and curricula. Thus this book was designed to save *you* personal, out-of-pocket expenses. Couldn't your hard-earned income be better spent on professional enrichment classes, having more pocket money, or even taking a summer vacation?

While compiling this book, my coauthor and I honestly found it thrilling to discover corporations (and meet the very "real" people at those corporations) that are starting up or running ongoing business-education collaborations. Corporations are genuinely enthusiastic about the process of being involved with a large-goal societal project. One executive (this one at Tic-Tac's Literacy Program, though the thought was echoed by others as well) remarked, "What a joy it is to take the seed of an idea and watch it grow, further a concept and make it a reality, and experience the rewards of helping others as we build multiple aspects of our business." Luckily, business-education collaboration is a two-way street. It benefits corporations as well—so well that corporate-sponsored community services and corporate donations are fast-growing, leading-edge phenomena.

As you work your way through this book, you will find many leading-edge companies that have discovered a new concept of profit and loss. Take the northern California fast-food Mexican restaurant chain that became so successful it was able to provide Saturday-morning English classes as well as management training and excellent wages to its workers. From the hard-nosed business perspective, the company could afford to provide such community resources because it made a profit . . . but one could just as easily say the company made a profit because it reinvested in the community. It created mutual trust by supporting the community, which, in turn, supports the company.

The companies and programs in this book believe in investing resources wisely and passing the benefits along to upcoming generations. And it is through learning in this improved context that kids just may discover areas and issues that are meaningful to them, do things that help others, or discover their own passions and path in life.

We hope this book will help you foster creativity and independent thinking in the classroom. Our rapidly changing times continually require us to learn new concepts. Creativity is more than a tool for the arts; it is a way of thinking that inspires the ability to turn ideas on their head, try new methods, and look for brand-new answers. Learning to think creatively allows children to grow up and forge a life that precludes futility and encompasses the desire for more than material goods. Your own creativity is at the heart of using *Unbelievably Good Deals That You Absolutely Can't Get Unless You're a Teacher*; this is not so much a book as it is a directory of connections waiting to be made.

As a teacher, you lead a giving life, and, paradoxically, you receive so much by giving. Right now you may be teaching a boy or girl who will one day discover how to cure cancer, stop war, clean up a river, and lead a productive and caring life that isn't devoid of hope. The power to change is clearly obtainable to us all. We build the future of our desires by the content of our efforts.

Certainly teachers teach students, mentors teach followers, grandparents teach grandchildren, uncles mentor nephews, kids can teach things to their parents, and icons and role models inspire and, hence, "teach" values. You see my point. There is a universality to this idea, and this universality makes this book appropriate for everyone everywhere.

Run into the future, building as you go. Take care of yourself and the person next to you. We're already on our way.

Here's wishing hope, peace, and understanding to us all.

—BH

Acknowledgments

Thanks to Ray Bradbury for the gentle insistence that I shout down my own well, and for the vision created in "The Toynbee Convector." May this book be a small step of which Craig Bennett Stiles would approve.

Thanks to William G. Thompson, Gene Brissie, Kathy Willhoite, Betsy Lancefield, Craig Bolt, Ed Stambaugh, Vivian Hamilton, David Russ, Jean Lyford, John Campos, Barbara Crawford, Chris Nelder, Nathan Henderson, Carmen Arjona, Thomas R. Zappelli, and the Ken Santoro family—Nicholas, Daniel, and especially Tracy, for her ceaseless and immeasurable support.

Special thanks to the Human Corporation—John, Paul, and George—for the influence and support.

To Nile Godfrey, whose support, friendship, and courage to make leading-edge ideas a reality helped illuminate the philanthropic path.

To Jon Anderson, with love. The holding doors *did* open. I turned around and *you* were standing close to *me*.

Thanks to Peter Gabriel, Annie Parsons, and David Stephen at Real World, and Deborah Heathersay and Thomas Brooman at WOMAD, for the open-minded conversations that afforded insight into your amazing and wonderful global and multicultural ventures.

For being touchstones and good friends, thanks to my nephews and niece, Dustin, Jason, Joshua, and Sara Harrington.

Deepest appreciation and love to Carly Simon, for the friendship and professionalism, and for reminding me you can always white-knuckle life if you have to.

To Jackie Miskel, proprietor of Bonanza Street Books, in Walnut Creek, California, and Bonanza Books, in Clayton, California, for friendship and tremendous support.

To Bill Downey, a great man who I was deeply saddened to hear had passed away. Bill was a consultant to me via the Santa Barbara Writer's Conference and gave validation to a then-young writer. Without him, I may not have gone on to publish the book you are now reading. Bill Downey encouraged my professionalism and tolerated my ambition. You are missed, Bill.

To some fine people who brought me back from the netherworld after a car wreck with a drunk driver: Andrew Knives, M.D.; Masem Mathias, M.D.; Howard Conklin, M.D.; Brian Candell, M.D.; Thomas Donovan, M.D.; Ken Jenner, attorney-at-law; Rev. Bruce Smith; Randall Starkey, M.D.; and many other people who helped ensure that I didn't suffer an even darker head injury.

And to Erik Torjeson, *il miglior fabbro*, who helped me find my way back by discussing how dark events go full circle back into positivity.

—BH

Chapter One

The Positive Classroom

REWARDS AND RESOURCES

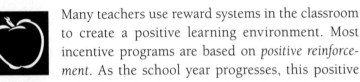 Many teachers use reward systems in the classroom to create a positive learning environment. Most incentive programs are based on *positive reinforcement*. As the school year progresses, this positive reinforcement should evolve from extrinsic motivation to intrinsic motivation as the reward systems ultimately teach children the desire to be rewarded *by their own achievement*. In this chapter, you will find many varieties of reward systems. Rewards can be tangible items (like toys, school supplies, and treats) or the less tangible—but just as coveted—like free time or a chance to play a game. (See the next section for a list of reward ideas.) A student's reward for reaching a goal can be a simple acknowledgment of the accomplishment or a more complex and creative function like creating a Treasure Chest or School Store, or scheduling a Room Party. Simply put, rewards acknowledge any kind of good behavior: helping others with work, keeping busy if finished early, not wasting time, keeping quiet when needed, *showing incentive*.

These programs can work only if concurrent work is being done on self-esteem; for learning to occur, kids need to feel positive about themselves and know they have abilities. (See the end of this chapter for tips on building self-esteem in your students.)

1

A reward system is not only an effective classroom tool, but it can be fun and rewarding for students and teachers alike.

Some Reward Systems You Can Use

Targeting Specific Behavior and Paying Compliments

A reward can simply be saying "Thank you" or "Good job" to a student for a good effort or job well done. But target specific behavior with your compliment: "Good report," "This was very well written," "Thank you for sitting quietly."

Incentive Programs

Incentive programs are excellent reward systems that combine extrinsic motivation and intrinsic motivation. A fairly uncomplicated incentive program is a "Fifty Stars Chart": use star stickers on an incentive chart. A student who receives fifty stars is given some form of prize or reward. Also see the "Book It!" reading charts in Other Organizations and Programs in Chapter 2.

"Caught Being Good" Slip

"Catch" children in good behavior (helping others, sharing, and so on) in the classroom, hall, or at recess, and reward them with a "Caught Being Good" slip that can be turned in to the office at the end of the day in return for a small prize.

Good Group Work/Good Day

Award entire groups (however you group children—cooperative learning groups or project groups, for example) for staying on task. Offer a points reward system, and at the end of the day, give a small prize to the group with the highest points.

The Marble System

Reward good class behavior by putting a couple of marbles in a jar, and promise students that when the jar is filled they may have a party. When the jar is filled, schedule a party (most likely for the final hour or two of a school day), and let your students plan it. They decide between choices you offer, for instance a video or free time. Ask each student to bring a favorite food or drink to share with the entire class.

Raffle Tickets

Present raffle tickets to children or groups for showing responsibility in their work. Reward good behavior such as staying on task, coming in from recess or lunch, and beginning work without having to be told. Present a raffle ticket to everyone who is doing well. Have them sign their names on the backs of the tickets, and put the tickets in a raffle box. Set up a time to draw the tickets (be it every week or every month) from the box—the reward is a trip to the Treasure Chest, described next.

Treasure Chest

The Treasure Chest is simply a chest full of prizes. You can build your own chest (taking a tip from pirate chests of yore) or purchase an inexpensive cardboard chest from your local novelty or party store. (See the next section for reward ideas to fill the chest.) Use the chest in conjunction with raffle tickets.

School Store

The School Store is similar to the Treasure Chest. One of the ways this system can work is to reward good behavior by giving points. Keep your record of the students' points in your roll book; they can keep track of their points as well. Be creative in designing whatever point system you see fit. Then create a School Store.

This store can be visible—that is, in a corner of your room, or in an empty space such as an unused classroom or old audio-visual room (several teachers might combine to "open" a larger store). Or you can simply create a small "catalog" (a sheet listing goodies, which is posted near your desk). An example of a system is listed here:

10 points = small prizes such as a sucker or stickers
20 points = paperback book
30 points = a game or some free time
40 points = a popular tape or CD
50 points = a popular video

Variation on School Store: The Super Store!

With perseverance, you may be able to form a partnership with a major corporation that could help you to stock your store with high-ticket items, such as software, CD–ROMs, and playground equipment. With such expensive items as prizes, you may have to change your system to distinguish between personal items (a game or software package awarded to a student) and donation items (gifts such as playground equipment that your kids work together to earn and donate to the school—complete with a plaque containing your class's name and the year the donation was earned).

Treats

Treats can be awarded for achieving one goal with the entire class. This of course varies according to age group, but sample ideas include:

- forming good lines every day for a week
- getting through an assignment
- staying on task
- overall good behavior

You can bake or buy brownies or other fun and nutritious foods. The reward could even be a cooking hour in which you teach a nutrition unit and eat the fruits of your labor.

Theme Parties

The same system with a similar prize (treats or cooking units) can be used throughout the year. Cook a turkey and bring it to class to teach about and celebrate Thanksgiving (or any and all special holidays and occasions). Acknowledge birthdays and new students in a similar fashion.

Speakers and Other Visitors

Treats come in many shapes and sizes. Speakers and visitors are another type of treat you can provide for your classroom, if your classroom earns it.

Free Time

Another reward is "free time" during which kids work on an in-classroom project. You may have a computer project or an art project on which they wish to put some extra time, or computer games might be available. Free time could also be used for an extracurricular activity or unit such as Storytelling Time or Music Appreciation. (Classical music is very calming to students.)

Recess

Recess, the old standby, is still a favorite.

Rewards

Obviously, to carry out the above reward systems, you need some tangible rewards. Choosing the right rewards may be more of an art than you would think, with changing tastes and the latest fads dictating what is "cool" and "in." But you will certainly get a sense of what your kids like and don't want rather quickly.

The majority of the rewards will be tokens that you can purchase economically at discount stores or shopping warehouses, keeping an eye out for off-season bargains. Of course it is what you do with the rewards (how they are presented and used to motivate) that makes them exciting. You might also want to order rewards from the companies listed in the next section. Specific reward ideas follow. This list will of course need to be adapted for the age group.

stickers

special pencils, crayons,
    markers

toys

books

games

special fun foods (e.g.,
    jelly beans, snack
    mixes, suckers, candy,
    bubble gum)

key chains

small bouncing balls

imitation money

hats

kimonos

cars

puzzles

certificates

trophies

ribbons

flashlights

bumperstickers

T-shirts

rubber stamps

pop CDs or cassettes

shoelaces

friendship bracelets

jewelry

baseball cards (and other
    sports cards: NFL,
    NBA, NHL)

comic books

bookmarks

erasers

stuffed animals

book covers

Kool-Aid packets and
    sodas

magazines

binders

folders

coin purses

rubber monsters
    (e.g., dinosaurs)

novelty items

bubbles

notepads

paints

magnets

paper dolls

posters

models

Reward Resources

Note: In listing these companies, we have (when appropriate) listed some of the many reward products they offer. We hope that these listings not only give you a clear idea of what you can obtain from a particular company, but also help provide a clearer sense of effective reward items—and help further stimulate your imagination along these lines.

Mail-Order Companies

THE COMPLETE COLLEGIATE AND THE COMPLETE TRAVELER

490 Route 46 East

Fairfield, NJ 07004

(201) 808-9249

■ The Complete Collegiate is a mail-order company featuring materials that can be used for rewards for lower grades, yet also has items for college students and travelers.

Ask for: See itemized list.

Requirements: See itemized list.

- Telephone book key chain. $1.50 plus self-addressed, stamped envelope (SASE).
- Identification tags. 3 for $1.25 plus SASE.
- Clown pen necklace. $1.25 plus SASE.
- Sticks on stones. 4 for $1.00 plus SASE.
- Neon wrist purse (perfect for lunch money). $1.25 plus SASE.
- "Financing Your Child's Education" (A slide rule guide packed with information).
- "Dorm Essentials Checklist" plus free "Complete Collegiate Catalog." Free with a business-size SASE.

DANORS

Wholesale-Souvenirs-Toys-Jewelry

5721 Funston Street, Bay 14

Hollywood, FL 33023

(954) 989-7550

Ask for: See itemized list.

Requirements: See itemized list.

- Purple shell necklace. Made in the Philippines of genuine seashells. $1.00 plus SASE.
- Monkey key ring. Five piece set of replica U.S. currency on a key ring. $1.00 plus SASE.

- 60 water balloons. $1.00 plus SASE.
- Pencil with 5-inch alligator on the end. $1.00 plus SASE.
- Carved pink shell ring. Made in the Philippines from real shell. $1.00 plus SASE.
- Colorful Florida magnet. $1.00 plus SASE.
- Click pencil. Use the pencil and click out a new point when needed. 7 new points. $1.00 plus SASE.
- Orange slice eraser. 2 for $1.00 plus SASE.
- Large alligator eraser. Over 3½ inches long. 75¢ plus SASE.
- NFL football trading cards. Pack of 14 different players. 75¢ plus SASE.
- Baseball trading cards. Pack of 14 different cards. 75¢ plus SASE.
- Basketball trading cards. Pack of 14 different cards. $.75 plus SASE.
- Hockey trading cards. Pack of 14 different cards. 75¢ plus SASE.
- Three colorful dinosaur erasers. $1.00 plus SASE.
- Prismatic stickers. 8 to 10 pieces per pack. Parrots, fish, shells, alligators. 2 packs for $1.00 plus SASE.
- Troll key ring. 75¢ plus SASE.
- Florida squeeze coin purse. $1.00 plus SASE.

HICKS SPECIALTIES

1308 68th Lane North
Brooklyn Center, MN 55430
(612) 566-9722

■ Company provides items at little or no cost.

Ask for: See itemized list.

Requirements: See itemized list.

- State stamp magnets (all states and District of Columbia are available). Please include 75¢ postage and handling.
- Disney stamp magnets (many characters and countries available). Please include 75¢ postage and handling.

- Boy Scout or Girl Scout stamp magnets. Please include 75¢ postage and handling.

INSTRUCTIONAL FAIR, INC.—T. S. DENISON
P.O. Box 1650
Grand Rapids, MI 49501
(800) 443-2976

■ Not a free resource (though they have terrific special sale items and will send you a free catalog), but a great overall resource nonetheless. Their products are available at school supply stores; call (800) 253-5469 to find the school supply store nearest you that carries Instructional Fair products. They sell record books, "Books I Have Read" charts, reward seals, badges (e.g., "I Had A Good Day," "Super Worker," "Student of the Day," "Computer Whiz," "Super Reader," gold and silver foil "medals." They also have whole language theme units, hands-on resource books, award certificates and awards in French, Japanese, and Spanish as well as English.

Ask for: Catalog.

Requirements: None.

PARKER FLAGS & PENNANTS
1001 N. Federal Highway, #30
Hallandale, FL 33009
(954) 454-0600; fax: (954) 458-7022

■ Parker Flags & Pennants was founded in 1950, and has since expanded to include a mail-order business that offers free items provided you send a business-size SASE and $1.00 for handling. They feature all types of flags, bumper strips, and souvenirs. Their materials (for example, a "The South Will Rise Again" bumper strip, a replica of an 1881 stock certificate, and early 1900 replica magazine ads) are good visuals and hands-on items for American history lessons. Likewise, their state decals are a good introduction to teaching the states.

Ask for: Product sheet or any specific item above.

Requirements: Business-size SASE and $1.00 for handling.

Publications

FREEBIES MAGAZINE
1135 Eugenia Place
Carpinteria, CA 93014-5025
(805) 566-1225; fax: (805) 566-0305

■ *Freebies* magazine is published five times a year and features fun items (not limited to educational resources) for $2.00 and less. Some of the items make excellent rewards and gifts. A fun activity may involve kids sending for the freebies on their own.

Ask for: Year subscription.

Requirements: Payment of $8.95—or $4.95 if you use the coupon in the back of their book (see following Lowell House Juvenile entry).

INFORMATION USA, INC.
P.O. Box E
Kensington, MD 20895
(800) UNCLESAM; fax: (301) 929-8907

■ Matthew Lesko's company features *Lesko's Info-Power II* and *1,001 Free Goodies and Cheapies*. The books are not *free*, but they will point you in the direction of government freebies. The information is not limited to education—not by any stretch of the imagination. But Lesko is a fun read, and one can uncover many government programs via his books.

Ask for: Information on Lesko's books.

Requirements: While the books are not free, you can obtain free information on these materials by calling the 800 number.

LOWELL HOUSE JUVENILE
2020 Avenue of the Stars, Suite 300
Los Angeles, CA 90067
(310) 552-7555; fax: (310) 552-7573

■ Publishes books *The Official Freebies for Kids* and *The Official Freebies for Teachers* by the editors of *Freebies* magazine. Contains reward, gift, and activity items.

Ask for: Best way to obtain book.

Requirements: Inexpensive book cost.

MEADOWBROOK PRESS
5451 Smetana Drive
Minnetonka, MN 55343
(612) 473-5400; fax: (612) 930-1940

■ Publishes *Free Stuff for Kids* and *More Free Stuff for Kids*. Quality rewards (stickers, supplies, multicultural items) and free information that can be very helpful as educational resources.

Ask for: Best way to obtain book.

Requirements: Inexpensive book cost.

PERIGEE BOOKS
The Putnam Publishing Group
200 Madison Avenue
New York, NY 10016
(212) 951-8400; fax: (212) 951-8993

■ *Free and Almost Free Things for Teachers* by Susan Osborn is published by Perigee and is a good source of educational resources for $5.00 and under.

Ask for: Information on where you can obtain books (or call your local bookstore).

Requirements: Currently under $5.00!

Other Sources

U.S. CHESS FEDERATION
186 Route 9W
New Windsor, NY 12553
(914) 562-8350

■ Few games are as exciting in the classroom as the ancient game of chess. If your high-tech-generation kids doubt this, rent the movie *Searching for Bobby Fischer*. Knowledge of chess develops and strengthens critical thinking and problem-solving skills. But, more to the point of this chapter on the positive classroom, chess can be an excellent reward—either to give away time for chess or to give away any number of chess-related items like boards or chess information.

Ask for: The catalog and a copy of Basic Chess Curriculum is free for the asking. You may also request *A Guide to Scholastic Chess*, a free booklet containing valuable information on organizing scholastic chess clubs; *Chess for Youth*, which provides free starter packages of chess sets and boards to help school programs get started; *Chess Coach Newsletter*, which provides current news and information concerning scholastic chess programs across the country, and organizational and promotional tips from successful chess coaches; and other free promotional material.

Requirements: Request on school letterhead when possible. Items listed under "Helping You Get Started" are free; items under "Basis for a Solid Program" are available for $30.00 (check payable to U.S. Chess Federation), when you include the name of an adult program sponsor, the school name, and the school address.

Building Students' Self-Esteem

1. Acknowledge and reassure your students.
2. Give specific praise.
3. Provide feedback on work.
4. Share feelings honestly.
5. Listen to your students.
6. Respect your students and teach them to respect you and each other.
7. Greet your students at the door each day.

8. Make structure part of the classroom. Set goals, make rules and post them, and plan activities for success.

9. Create posters, banners, and signs celebrating your goals, students, and diversity.

10. Go through visualizations and guided imagery with students. (Ask them to imagine a safe place, and imagine themselves in the future as balanced, successful people.)

11. Create a photo bulletin board by asking students to post baby photos, photos of home, and school photos. Throughout the year, add to this collection by taking photos of classroom activities. This action will offer the students a sense of belonging and ownership.

12. Phone students' homes in the first week. Make sure it is a positive call (establishing communication with parents that is different from "trouble" reports and negative calls to home). Make it a short, welcome call.

13. Send positive postcards home once or twice a week, emphasizing something positive about the student's week. Include everyone.

14. Record students' birthdays in your roll book and celebrate each one (a special birthday bulletin board, a card signed by the entire class, a treat with a candle, singing "Happy Birthday," etc.)

15. Put positive Post-it stickers around classroom.

16. Have students do a "Show and Tell" demonstration of something at which they excel.

17. Have students create "An Autobiographical Artwork," which could be a poster, T-shirt, collage, story, or Box Movie (see sidebar). Include the following: name, interests, hobbies, favorite music, favorite food, favorite sport (or team), accomplishments, and goals.

Teaching Positivity

POSITIVE COMMUNICATIONS, INC.

66 E. Main Street
Pawling, NY 12564
(914) 855-9600; fax: (914) 855-1036

■ The Positive Kids video series (for children in grades 2–4) will increase students' decision-making and problem-solving skills and greatly benefit your local school or community youth program.

Growing up in today's world is hard on children as they face many serious problems. The Positive Kids program helps children learn the skills and develop the positive attitude and self-esteem necessary for success in the classroom and in life. The video program is an award-winning series helping kids learn that problems can be solved and teaching them specific problem-solving techniques . . . all in a fun and entertaining way.

The four videos in this program feature live-action sequences of real elementary students solving their own real-life problems. Cartoon animation and creative puppetry keeps kids completely interested in learning how they, too, can solve problems. Children learn decision-making skills, learn to take responsibility for their own actions, to accept others, to understand their problems, to support peers, and to cope with the day-to-day challenges they face growing up. And the challenges they face are big ones—such as whether to get involved with or avoid alcohol and other drugs, peer pressure, crime, vandalism, and on and on. The program aims to teach children skills needed to make the right choices. The benefits of teaching positivity affect everyone:

- Kids see positive role models and effective problem solving in action. They'll be guided through step-by-step problem-solving sequences.
- Teachers are often thrilled by the approach to problem solving that their students learn from the program and how this approach creates a more positive learning environment.
- Principals will be pleased to hear that schools teaching positivity have reported improved playground behavior.

An Illustrated Activity: The Box Movie

The students' "An Autobiographical Artwork" can take the form of "The Box Movie." Have students make "movies" (storyboards) of their lives (where they were born, family, interests, hobbies), or have them detail interesting or unique aspects of their lives.

How to Make a Box Movie

Recycle a large laundry detergent box. Cut out the back and top and make a rectangle in the front (about the size and shape of a television screen). Collect two spools from empty paper towels. Find paper the size of your "screen." You'll also need pencils, pens, paints, markers, scissors, and tape. Create a movie made from a dozen or two dozen illustrated stills (drawings, magazine clippings, collage/mixed media work, or other colorful pictures). Attach the stills together via tape and connect them to paper towel spools. The student, a live narrator, scripts words on the back of the movie still illustration that correlates image and narrative. Wind the left spool to "play" the movie. Have students perform their stories.

Tips on Using Brainstorming and Clustering for Story Development

Have students create their story, and break the story into components. "My Hiking Adventure" could become these components: trip to national park, hiking to lake, discovering things in nature, discovering the land of the ancient Indian burial ground, hiking back to base camp, and eating pizza after wilderness camping for three days.

When students get this far, encourage them to continue to develop their story by brainstorming and clustering techniques. For example, "Discovering Things in

Nature" could become a series of mental associations, which could become story components, which then translate into movie stills:

Expand by listing *specific* "Things in Nature":

1. Bears
2. High mountains
3. Snake that scared my uncle
4. Fishing for dinner
5. Making our campfire from fallen trees
6. Swimming to rock island in the middle of the lake
7. History of area (battles that may have taken place there)

- Guidance counselors will appreciate that The National Office of Substance Abuse Prevention (OSAP) calls these programs "accurate" and "important." Many schools have used local, county, state, or federal drug prevention funds to purchase these videos. In some communities local clubs and civic organizations have purchased the programs for their schools.

Ask for: Free information on Positive Kids video program. Free preview tape for 30 days.

Requirements: Return the preview tape after 30 days. If interested in the program, special savings are available.

Chapter Two

Reading and Book Materials

"Reading builds vocabulary. Since words are symbols for ideas, the more words a child knows, the more ideas he or she has. And ideas are the soil in which creativity grows."

—JOHN GILE

 We encourage you to read through this section not just for "reading" materials or novel-based themes, but for books—those glorious information-packed tomes. Books (and, of course, educational magazines) often cover many subject areas that can be used across the curriculum—language arts, science, resource guides, math, social studies, multicultural books, ESL, life skills, and literacy.

Herein is a list of the nation's children's book publishers who are part of the Children's Book Council, as well as a list of applicable magazine publishers, and other organizations related to reading, books, and literature. (Of course these days "book" is beginning to mean other media beyond the "traditional format," media like CD-ROM or computer disks. We expand upon this new technology in Chapter 8, but touch upon it in this chapter.)

When you write to these publishers, you will, at the very least, obtain a free copy of their publishing program, usually in the form of a catalog. Explore this material, as the world of publishing—which includes a wide variety of formats including CD-ROMs, audiotapes, videos, and interactive software—offers an amazing array of products.

Quite often (depending upon the offer) the package of free materials or promotional items includes:

- publication catalogs
- biographical materials on the authors published
- book posters
- postcards
- teachers' guides
- activity kits
- information on teachers' discounts
- information on quantity discounts

When you begin to receive publishers' promotional materials, you will be pleased, perhaps amazed, at the wealth and quality of the materials. We urge you to start writing and establishing your contacts, and hope you enjoy the process . . . which can be fun as well as rewarding.

The Children's Book Council

THE CHILDREN'S BOOK COUNCIL (CBC)
568 Broadway, Suite 404
New York, NY 10012
(212) 966-1990; fax: (212) 966-2073

■ CBC is a nonprofit organization that encourages young people to read.

Ask for: New catalog.

Requirements: The free catalog offers quality posters, bookmarks, and informational resources at low prices. A one-time membership fee of $60.00 entitles the subscriber to the *CBC Features Newsletter* and catalog, twice a year—for life.

To obtain the CBC free and inexpensive materials enclose a self-addressed, stamped envelope with your order. Unless otherwise noted, the following materials all require a 6″ × 9″ envelope and 3 oz. first-class postage; contact your post office for current postage rates per ounce. If you are requesting more than one item, send a 6″ × 9″ SASE with the total postage required to cover all of the materials you want. The following are available:

- **CBC free catalog.** Lists reading promotion materials and ordering information.
- **CBC Features.** A sample of the semi-annual newsletter.
- **CBC Members' List including Members' Publishing Programs.** Contains members' names and addresses, key personnel, description of types of books published, the size of lists, and manuscript submission guidelines.
- **CBC Bookmark Sampler.** One copy of current CBC bookmarks.
- **How to Celebrate Book Week.** Tested ideas offered by teachers and librarians.
- **Inviting Children's Book Authors and Illustrators to Your Community.** A how-to guide for contacting authors and illustrators with listings (and contact names) of CBC-member publishers.
- **Notable Children's Trade Books in the Field of Social Sciences.** Bibliography of the year's best.
- **Outstanding Science Trade Books for Children.** Bibliography of the year's best.
- **Choosing a Child's Book.** Parents' education pamphlet for selecting books for children.
- **Children's Choices.** A bibliographic list issued by the International Reading Association (IRA)–CBC Joint Committee List of the year's most popular books, selected by 10,000 children nationwide. Send a 9″ × 12″ SASE (with 4-oz. first-class postage) to IRA at 800 Barksdale Road, P.O. Box 8139, Newark, DE 19714-8139.

- **13 Exciting Reading Activities for Children.** A pamphlet of fun, creative ways to get kids to read.
- **75 Authors and Illustrators Everyone Should Know.** A selection to introduce kids and adults to children's book writers and illustrators and their books.
- **Writing Children's Books.** Information for writers about children's book publishing.
- **Illustrating Children's Books.** Information for illustrators about children's book publishing.

Book Publishers

ACADEMIC THERAPY PUBLICATIONS (ATP)
High Noon Books
Ann Arbor Division
20 Commercial Boulevard
Novato, CA 94949-6191
(800) 422-7249; fax: (415) 883-3720

■ The High Noon Books Catalog contains high-interest, low-level books and learning materials for kids or adults who have reading difficulties. Adventuresome storylines and bright subject matter (imagine the ease of introducing a child to easy-reading books that feature teenagers in sports and mystery stories) are offered along with workbooks that help build reading comprehension skills, vocabulary, and more.

ATP also offers the *Directory of Facilities and Services for the Learning Disabled*, which is updated biannually and available for only $5.00 to cover postage and handling (bulk pricing is also available). This guide includes state-by-state listings of services and is a super resource for finding educational materials for special-needs kids and also for referring to specialists when outside help is needed.

Ask for: High Noon Books and ATP/Ann Arbor Catalogs. Free.

Requirements: None

ARTISTS & WRITERS GUILD BOOKS

Attn: Pamela Nadan
850 Third Avenue
New York, NY 10022
(212) 753-8500

Ask for: Catalog and promotional materials for your age group. Publishes books for preschool through early middle grades. Features picture books, pop-up, and specialty books.

Requirements: No particular requirements listed. Send postcard or mail request on school letterhead when possible.

BANTAM DOUBLEDAY DELL (BDD)
Books for Young Readers

School and Library Marketing
1540 Broadway
New York, NY 10036
(212) 354-6500; fax: (212) 782-8890

Ask for: Catalog and promotional materials (including author biographies) for your age group. BDD is a powerhouse publisher that has many imprints. A letter requesting appropriate catalogs will provide a treasure chest of publishing programs for preschool through young adult books. Their imprints include:

- Delacorte Press: fiction and nonfiction for middle grade and young adult readers.
- Doubleday Books for young readers: picture books.
- Picture Yearling: paperbacks (illustrated) for preschool through primary grades.
- Yearling: fiction for ages 8–12.
- Skylark: original paperbacks, ages 8–12.
- Laurel Leaf: fiction by well-known authors in paperback for ages 12 and up.
- Starfire: paperback originals for ages 12 and up.
- Rooster: novelty books and board books.
- Ghostwriter: for ages 7–10.

- The Saddle Club: novels, puzzle, and joke books for ages 8–11.
- Sweet Valley Kids: novels about girls and horses, for ages 6–9.
- Sweet Valley Twins: for ages 8–12.
- Sweet Valley High: for readers 10 and up.
- Sweet Valley University: for ages 12 and up.
- Bank Street: early readers, ages 4–8.
- Choose Your Own Adventure: for ages 10–14.
- Road to Avonlea: for ages 8–12.
- Sports Illustrated for Kids: for ages 8–12.

Requirements: None.

BEECH TREE BOOKS
1350 Avenue of the Americas
New York, NY 10019
(212) 261-6500; fax: (212) 261-6549

Ask for: Catalog and promotional materials for your age group. Beech Tree Books publishes paperback books for middle-grade and young adult readers. Their publishing program includes hands-on activity books, adventure stories, contemporary and historical fiction, and biographies, as well as books on health issues such as drug and alcohol abuse.

Requirements: No particular requirements listed. Send postcard or mail request on school letterhead when possible.

BRIDGEWATER BOOKS
100 Corporate Drive
Mahwah, NJ 07430
(201) 529-4000; fax: (201) 529-2781

Ask for: Catalog and promotional materials for your age group.

Requirements: No particular requirements listed. Send postcard or mail request on school letterhead when possible.

CAROLRHODA BOOKS, INC.
241 First Avenue North
Minneapolis, MN 55401
(612) 332-3344

Ask for: Call for catalog and promotional materials (e.g., bookmarks) for your age group. Publishes books for preschool through 6th grade. They feature picture books, and illustrated nonfiction and fiction. Samples of their educational line are:

- Earth Watch Science Books
- Nature Watch
- On My Own Beginning Readers
- Creative Minds Biographies
- Trailblazers Biographies
- Photo Essay Books

Requirements: No particular requirements listed. Send postcard or mail request on school letterhead when possible.

CHARLESBRIDGE PUBLISHING
85 Main Street
Watertown, MA 02172
(617) 926-0329; fax: (617) 926-5720

Ask for: Catalog and promotional materials for your age group. Books emphasize environmental and multicultural themes. Editions are also published in Spanish. Also ask for information on how you can be considered for their Damaged & Defective (D&D) program (see box).

Requirements: No particular requirements listed. Send postcard or mail request on school letterhead when possible.

CHILDREN'S BOOK PRESS
246 First State, Suite 101
San Francisco, CA 94105
(415) 995-2200; fax: (415) 995-2222

Ask for: Full-color poster (17″ × 22″) for current paperback reissues.

Requirements: 9″ × 12″ SASE with 3-oz. first-class postage.

CREATIVE EDUCATION, INC.
123 South Broad Street
Mankato, MN 56001
(507) 388-6273; fax: (507) 388-2746

Ask for: Catalog and promotional materials for your age group. Preschool through young adult. Picture nonfiction and fiction, and photo essays for all age groups.

Requirements: No particular requirements listed. Send postcard or mail request on school letterhead when possible.

CROWN PUBLISHERS
201 East 50th Street
New York, NY 10022
(212) 572-2600; fax: (212) 940-7868

Ask for: Catalog and promotional materials for your age group. Picture books, preschool, and young adult titles. Publishes both fiction and nonfiction.

Requirements: No particular requirements listed. Send postcard or mail request on school letterhead when possible.

Free Books for Teachers

Some publishers provide book samples, free of charge, to economically disadvantaged schools. These books are often gifts from publisher overruns, damaged and defective copies, and returns. Defective books are often new, beautiful, and interesting books. They're defective because they contain a mistake—a title that was printed wrong, or some other minor change. In no way are defective books bad. All inquiries have to be sent on a school purchase order or school letterhead. Requests for free material may not be made over the telephone, but must be either mailed or faxed to the publisher. In general, you can write to any of the publishers listed in this chapter and request your needs (e.g., two or three books for 6th-grade science). They will check their stock and try to provide an appropriate match as a gift to your school.

Ask for: Information on how you can be considered for their D&D program.

Requirements: Check with publisher to see if they have a D&D program. Specific requirements may vary according to the time of year and book availability. Make specific requests, but be prepared to accept substitutes. For example, you may request 25 copies of a class set and receive 24 copies of one book and one of another type . . . though you should brace for more extreme variations as well! A nominal charge of $1.00 for each softcover book and $2.00 for hardcover books covers shipping.

We also encourage you to write to publishers who don't have D&D programs—and strongly suggest they develop one! Explain the type of school in which you teach, and ask them if they ever give away gifts, publisher overruns, damaged and defective copies, or returns. Then ask not what this company can do for you, but what can you do for this company? Can you get several other teachers in on the deal and buy two or three classroom sets (30 to 90 copies) of another title they publish? Will your read-a-thon winners be published in the newspaper in front of a banner that reads KIDS-PRESS (or Lonely Planet, Wingbow Press, or Time Warner or whatever the name of their publishing company may be)? Remind them that you can help their public image (and live up to your end of the bargain, of course).

Remember, too, that a lot of these companies already donate on a local level, around their own hometowns. If someone can't always help you out, try to understand.

DIAL BOOKS FOR YOUNG READERS
(Penguin USA)
375 Hudson Street
New York, NY 10014
(212) 366-2800; fax: (212) 366-2020

Ask for: Catalog and promotional materials for your age group. List includes:

- Very First Books: toddlers
- Easy-to-Read: primary readers
- Preschool titles
- Young Adult titles
- Pied Piper Books: picture book reprints

Requirements: No particular requirements listed. Send postcard or mail request on school letterhead when possible.

DISCOVERY ENTERPRISES, LTD.
31 Laurelwood Drive
Carlisle, MA 01741
(800) 729-1720; fax: (508) 937-5779

Ask for: Catalog. Publishing program includes:

- Perspectives on History Series: primary source materials
- Picture-book Biography Series
- Classroom Plays: grades 4–8
- Curriculum Materials for Teachers: K–12
- Global Awareness Materials from Childreach: grades 3–6
- Coloring Books

Requirements: SASE with 2-oz. postage. Mail request on school letterhead when possible.

DISNEY PRESS
114 Fifth Avenue
New York, NY 10011
(212) 633-4400; fax: (212) 633-4833

Ask for: Catalog and promotional materials for your age group. Disney publishes a children's literature trade list, both in attractive hardcover and paperback. The fiction and nonfiction titles are based on characters from the classic Disney films (and television). Includes picture books, boards, novelty, and pop-ups from Disney's historical past.

Requirements: No particular requirements listed. Send postcard or mail request on school letterhead when possible.

DOVER PUBLICATIONS, INC.
31 East 2nd Street
Mineola, NY 11501
(516) 294-7000; fax: (516) 742-6953

■ Catalogs for Dover's books can be obtained, free of charge, by writing to the above address. Dover publishes high-quality paperback books in all fields, and features as well a Children's Book Catalog offering more than 900 books ranging mostly from $1.00 to $3.95. An outstanding one-stop resource for classics, cut & assemble, game and puzzle books, educational activity books, and paper dolls. Publishes more than 200 "Little Activity Books" for $1.00 each. Books can be purchased from local bookstores or directly from Dover Publications at the above address.

Ask for: Catalog.

Requirements: None.

DUTTON CHILDREN'S BOOKS
Penguin USA
375 Hudson Street
New York, NY 10014
(212) 366-2600; fax: (212) 366-2666

Ask for: Catalog and promotional materials for your age group. Dutton publishes a book list that includes preschool, picture books, young adult, novelty, pop-up, and fiction and nonfiction. Line includes:

• Unicorn paperbacks: picture book reprints
• Dutton Easy Readers: for beginning readers
• Dutton Speedsters: transitional beginner readers

Requirements: No particular requirements listed. Send postcard or mail request on school letterhead when possible.

FARRAR, STRAUS & GIROUX, INC.
Attn: Children's Marketing Department
19 Union Square West
New York, NY 10003
(212) 741-6900; fax: (212) 206-5340

Ask for: Catalog and promotional materials for your age group. Preschool through young adult titles are available. List includes picture books, and fiction and nonfiction. Their paperback line (which reprints their backlist) is Sunburst Books.

Special Offers from Discovery Enterprises, Ltd.

Author Tours

Discovery Enterprises offers a brochure on author tours called Meet an Author. Not only are Discovery Enterprises authors and illustrators available to talk to students about researching, writing, illustrating, and publishing books, but the valuable information Discovery Enterprises provides will also help you understand the process of holding such an event. For more information, call (800) 729-1720.

Childreach's Global Awareness Project

A hands-on social studies program for grades 3–6. Through Childreach (a division of the worldwide organization PLAN International), a classroom can sponsor a child in a developing country. The cost (payable by the PTA or by having each child in the class contribute a dollar) is $22.00 a month. This pays for a child's care (school, medicine, and parent education) in 32 countries in Africa, Asia, and Central and South America. The class can decide if they wish to sponsor a boy or girl, and will become pen-friends with the child. This activity also helps U.S. students realize that despite difficulties in America's toughest neighborhoods, they are still very fortunate. Kids also feel empowered by helping their less fortunate peers.

The innovative Kids for Kids Global Awareness Project is provided to the classroom free when they "adopt" a child. Childreach notes, "Each kit contains background information on the countries and 28 full-color activity sheets with informative articles on education, health, geography, lifestyles, environmental issues, and more.

Activity sheets may be photocopied for classroom use. Students may send in their [activity] projects for possible publication in the national Kids for Kids newsletter."

The classroom also receives a Multidisciplinary Curriculum Package including a teacher's guide, student activity sheets, and laminated photographs and artwork from children in developing countries along with school or classroom sponsorship, called See Me, Share My World.

Requirements: No particular requirements listed. Send postcard or mail request on school letterhead when possible.

FREDERICK WARNE & CO., INC.

Penguin USA
375 Hudson Street
New York, NY 10014
(212) 366-2000; fax: (212) 366-2666

Ask for: Catalog and promotional materials for your age group. List includes hardcovers, paperbacks, novelties, and pop-ups. Classic children's authors include:

- Beatrix Potter
- Kathleen Hale
- Cicely Mary Barker

Requirements: No particular requirements listed. Send postcard or mail request on school letterhead when possible.

FREE SPIRIT PUBLISHING

400 First Avenue North, Suite 616
Minneapolis, MN 55401-1724
(612) 338-2068; fax: (612) 337-5050

■ Very supportive of children and their rights. Among their excellent publications are *The Kid's Guide to Social Action* and the *Directory of American Youth Organizations.*

Ask for: Free Spirit Catalog.

Requirements: None.

HARCOURT BRACE AND COMPANY
525 B Street, Suite 1900
San Diego, CA 92101-4495
(619) 699-6435; fax: (619) 699-6777

Ask for: Catalog and promotional materials for your age group. Publishing program includes preschool through young adult. List includes Gulliver Green Books (environmental books, widely used by teachers, that include works by Lynne Cherry) and Magic Carpet Books (a new line of fantasy for for young readers available in affordable paperback editions).

In addition, teachers and students are invited to join the Greenpatch Kids Club, an alliance of young people who want to learn about the environment and how to protect it. Titles in the series of books include *Big Bugs, Nightprowlers, Dirty Rotten Dead?,* and *You Animal!* All titles include activities and case studies about real children who are making a difference in our environment.

Requirements: SASE with $2.00 postage. Mail request on school letterhead when possible.

GIBBS SMITH
P.O. Box 667
Layton, UT 84041
(801) 544-9800; fax: (801) 544-5582;
website: www.gibbs-smith.com

■ Gibbs Smith is a top-quality trade publisher that produces a variety of books, including children's activity books for ages four and up. These quality books are educational, beautiful, and lots of fun. Favorite children's titles include *Mapped Out!, The Search for Snookums, Paper Making for Kids, Eric Van Noodel,* and *Sleeping in a Sack.*

Gibb Smith has a significant number of free deals. Write to the address above to request periodic promotional materials such as bookmarks and posters. They have a small D&D program and an author appearance program.

Ask for: Free catalogs, promotional materials, and/or information on D&D and the author appearance programs.

Requirements: Please mail requests on school letterhead.

GOOD BOOKS
Main Street
P.O. Box 419
Intercourse, PA 17534
(717) 768-7171; fax: (717) 768-3433

Ask for: Catalog and promotional materials for your age group. Hardcover and paperback titles include picture books, fiction, and how-to for grades 3–6 and 4–10.

Requirements: None.

GREENWILLOW BOOKS
1350 Avenue of the Americas
New York, NY 10019
(212) 261-6500; fax: (212) 261-6619

Ask for: Catalog and promotional materials for your age group.

Requirements: No particular requirements listed. Send postcard or mail request on school letterhead when possible.

GROLIER, INC.
90 Sherman Turnpike
Danbury, CT 06816
(800) 621-1115 or (203) 797-3500; fax: (305) 797-3123

Ask for: Catalog and promotional materials for your age group (grades 4–12). Emphasizes nonfiction subject areas of social studies, technology, and science.

Requirements: No particular requirements listed. Send postcard or mail request on school letterhead when possible.

GROSSET & DUNLAP, INC.
200 Madison Avenue
New York, NY 10016
(212) 951-8400; fax: (212) 213-6706

Ask for: Catalog and promotional materials for your age group.
Publishes Platt & Munk titles.

Requirements: No particular requirements listed. Send postcard
or mail request on school letterhead when possible.

HARPERCOLLINS CHILDREN'S BOOKS
10 East 53rd Street
New York, NY 10022
(212) 207-7044; fax: (212) 207-7996

Ask for: Catalog and promotional materials for your age group.

Requirements: No particular requirements listed. Send postcard
or mail request on school letterhead when possible.

HARPER TROPHY PAPERBACKS
(HarperCollins Children's Books)
10 East 53rd Street
New York, NY 10022
(212) 207-7044; fax: (212) 207-7996

Ask for: Catalog and promotional materials for your age group.

Requirements: No particular requirements listed. Send postcard
or mail request on school letterhead when possible.

HENRY HOLT AND COMPANY, INC.
115 West 18th Street
New York, NY 10011
(212) 886-9200; fax: (212) 633-0748

Ask for: Catalog and promotional materials for your age group.

Requirements: No particular requirements listed. Send postcard
or mail request on school letterhead when possible.

HOUGHTON MIFFLIN CO.
222 Berkeley Street
Boston, MA 02116
(617) 351-5000; fax: (617) 351-1100

Ask for: Catalog and promotional materials for your age group.

Requirements: No particular requirements listed. Send postcard or mail request on school letterhead when possible.

HYPERION BOOKS FOR CHILDREN
Attn: Linda Lewis or Lisa Ann Fink
114 Fifth Avenue
New York, NY 10011
(212) 633-4400; fax: (212) 807-5432

Ask for: Classroom ideas brochure. Hyperion Books for Children has an innovative catalog that is also a teacher's activity guide. In it, the publisher acknowledges the fact that literature is becoming the centerpiece of learning in the classroom across the curriculum. The ideas and activities in this catalog, each of which parallels a book, are from teachers across Canada and the United States. Hyperion puts it best: "[The activities] are starting places for you and are meant to stimulate your own ideas." If you do indeed obtain this catalog and expand upon these suggestions, they invite you to share your ideas by writing to Lauren Wohl at the above address. *Highly recommended.*

Requirements: Send a 9″ × 12″ SASE with 20-oz. first-class postage.

IDEALS CHILDREN'S BOOKS
Hambleton-Hill Publishing
1501 County Hospital Road
Nashville, TN 37218
(615) 254-2480; fax: (615) 254-2405

Ask for: Catalog and promotional materials for your age group. Publishes hardcover and paperback children's literature. Age range includes preschool through sixth grade. Products feature picture books, and fiction and nonfiction, hands-on activities, novelty, board, and library books.

Requirements: None.

JOY STREET BOOKS

Little, Brown & Co.
3 Center Plaza
Boston, MA 02108-2084
(617) 227-0730 or (800) 759-0190

Ask for: Catalog and promotional materials for your age group. Hardcover and paperback children's literature, preschool through young adult. List includes picture books and fiction and nonfiction. Growing publication in nonfiction for the 8–12 set.

Requirements: No particular requirements listed. Send postcard or mail request on school letterhead when possible.

ALFRED A. KNOPF, INC.

201 East 50th Street
New York, NY 10022
(212) 572-2600; fax: (212) 572-8700

Ask for: Catalog and promotional materials for your age group.

Requirements: No particular requirements listed. Send postcard or mail request on school letterhead when possible.

LERNER PUBLICATIONS COMPANY

241 First Avenue North
Minneapolis, MN 55401
(800) 328-4929 or (612) 332-3344; fax: (612) 332-7615

Ask for: Catalog and promotional materials for your age group. Emphasis on educational books for ages 7–18. Fiction titles, mysteries, and novels on multicultural themes are targeted for middle grades. Nonfiction subjects include social issues, biography, science and technology, history, the environment, sports, entertainment, the arts, crafts, and activities.

Requirements: None.

LITTLE, BROWN & CO.

3 Center Plaza
Boston, MA 02108-2084
(617) 227-0730

■ Established in 1837 and publishes a variety of books, including lavishly illustrated children's books. Each publishing season the children's publicity department produces promotional posters, bookmarks, and postcards that correspond to specific new titles. The items are free, but change too frequently to itemize. Also available are a variety of "teacher tips" brochures and author biographies. For membership in the Matt Christopher Fan Club, send a check for $1 in a business-size envelope to the Matt Christopher Fan Club at the above address.

Ask for: Catalog and promotional materials for your age group.

Requirements: No particular requirements listed (note requirement for the Matt Christopher Fan Club). Send postcard or mail request on school letterhead when possible.

LODESTAR BOOKS

Dutton/Penguin
375 Hudson Street
New York, NY 10014
(212) 366-2627; fax: (212) 366-2666

Ask for: Catalog and promotional materials for your age group.

Requirements: No particular requirements listed. Send postcard or mail request on school letterhead when possible.

LOTHROP, LEE & SHEPARD BOOKS

Attn: CBMD
1350 Avenue of the Americas
New York, NY 10019
(212) 261-6500; fax: (212) 261-6595

Ask for: *Down Buttermilk Lane* poster.

Requirements: Self-addressed label with 3-oz. first-class postage.

 **Free Sample of Folk Tales**

Eight classic stories are transformed in this Musicraft production. Easy songs with stick puppet cutouts are offered as a free sample for you to try. Call Memphis Musicraft, (800) 595-6732.

THE MILLBROOK PRESS, INC.
2 Old New Milford Road
Brookfield, CT 06804
(203) 740-2220; fax: (203) 740-2526

Ask for: Catalog and promotional materials for your age group. Preschool through young adult. Titles are primarily picture books, nonfiction, and reference works and library books.

Requirements: No particular requirements listed. Send postcard or mail request on school letterhead when possible.

MILLIKEN PUBLISHING COMPANY
Publishers of Educational Material
1100 Research Boulevard
P.O. Box 21579
St. Louis, MO 63132-0579
(314) 991-4220 or (800) 325-4136;
fax: (314) 991-4807 or (800) 538-1319

Ask for: Information on how you can be considered for their D&D program.

Requirements: Specific requirements may vary according to the time of year and book availability.

MULBERRY BOOKS

Attn: Lori Benton
1350 Avenue of the Americas
New York, NY 10019
(212) 261-6792; fax: (212) 261-6785

■ Ask about the Mulberry Big Book program. The Big Book program provides preschool and primary grade levels with proven classroom favorites in oversized formats. Perhaps most compelling of all is the fact that a teacher's guide comes with every Big Book featuring guidelines such as "Meet the Book," "Read the Book," "Extend the Book," "Things to Think and Talk About," "Things to Write About," and "Make Connections Across the Curriculum." Teachers' Guides are also available separately. (If you purchased a Mulberry Book from a bookstore, you can still call the publisher who will send you the guide.) If unable to obtain books from your local bookseller or wholesaler, call customer service at (800) 237-0657 for ordering information.

Ask for: 25 bookmarks featuring Mulberry Read-Alone titles.

Requirements: Send self-addressed 9″ label with 3-oz. first-class postage.

NORTH-SOUTH BOOKS

1123 Broadway, Suite 800
New York, NY 10010
(212) 463-9736; fax: (212) 633-1004

Ask for: Catalog and promotional materials for your age group. Picture books and nonfiction titles. North-South Books is the English imprint of Nord-Sud Verlag, Switzerland.

Requirements: No particular requirements listed. Send postcard or mail request on school letterhead when possible.

ORCHARD BOOKS
95 Madison Avenue
New York, NY 10016
(212) 951-2600; fax: (212) 213-6435

Ask for: Catalog and promotional materials for your age group.

Requirements: Make letter as specific as possible If you order a catalog, can you define which catalog? If you need promotional materials, can you list which authors interest you most? If you just want bookmarks and some basic promotional materials but are not sure of the specifics, they will still field your request. Orchard Books also publishes excellent multicultural books.

And please don't forget your return address.

PELICAN PUBLISHING COMPANY, INC.
200 Newton
P.O. Box 3110
Gretna, LA 70054
(504) 368-1175; fax: (504) 368-1195

Ask for: Catalog and promotional materials for your age group. Publishes books for lower elementary, junior high to young adult.

Requirements: No particular requirements listed. Send postcard or mail request on school letterhead when possible.

PHILOMEL BOOKS & PUTNAM BOOKS
Putnam & Grosset Group
200 Madison Avenue
New York, NY 10016
(212) 951-8773; fax: (212) 213-6706

Ask for: Catalog and promotional materials for your age group.

Requirements: Send requests to Institutional Sales Department at above address, attn: Jennifer Abcug.

PLEASANT COMPANY

8400 Fairway Place
P.O. Box 991
Middleton, WI 53562
Attn: Julie J. Parks, Public Relations Coordinator
(800) 233-0264 or (800) 845-0005; fax: (608) 836-0761

Ask for: Catalog and promotional materials for your age group. Featured titles and/or series include:

- The American Girls Collection®: 36 different titles of historical fiction for girls, ages 7–12. Each book features a nine-year-old girl's life in a different period of American history—1774, 1824, 1854, 1864, 1904, 1944—and concludes with a nonfiction picture essay, *Looking Back*, that further explores the character's historical period.
- American Girls Pastimes™: 20 activity books filled with projects from the past for girls of today. Cookbooks, craft books, theater kits, and paper dolls, featuring the characters in The American Girls Collection, offers girls the chance to recreate activities from different periods in America's past.
- American Girl Library®: Contemporary advice and activity books that capture the spirit of today's American girl. The lively collection of books is inspired by the most popular departments of *American Girl®* magazine.
- America At School™: A curriculum unit designed for grades 3–5 that integrates history, social studies, language arts, and literature. Based on the popular school stories from The American Girls Collection, the unit examines education during five important historical periods in American history.
- Teacher's Guides: This series helps teachers more effectively use the books from The American Girls Collection. Each guide focuses on one of the characters in the Collection and offers background on her historical period, along with plot and theme summaries of the 6 books in the series.
- *Five Plays: Teacher's Guide and Scripts*: Features American Girls plays for classroom use. Includes reproducible play scripts,

background notes, reproducible production tips, and improvisational drama activities to reinforce important themes.

Requirements: No particular requirements listed. Send postcard or mail request on school letterhead when possible. Educators can call (800) 350-6555 for a free school and library catalog. Educator rates reflect a 20 percent discount from standard consumer prices.

PORTUNUS PUBLISHING COMPANY
3445 Ocean Park Boulevard, Suite 203
Santa Monica, CA 90405

Ask for: Catalog and promotional materials for your age group; publishes books for readers ranging from preschool to young adult. Subject matter includes illustrated concept books, fiction, special-interest books, adventure stories, and biographies.

Requirements: No particular requirements listed. Send postcard or mail request on school letterhead when possible.

PUFFIN BOOKS
Penguin Putnam, Inc.
375 Hudson Street
New York, NY 10014
(212) 366-2295; fax: (212) 366-2012

■ Puffin Books has developed a club as a service to teachers. Through it, the publicity department provides free promotional items for classrooms four times a year. There is never any charge to belong to the club and the materials are always complimentary. No purchases are required, although deeply discounted book sets are also offered.

Ask for: Puffin Teacher Club and *Puffin Papers* newsletter (see further details below).

Requirements: To sign up for the Puffin Teacher's Club, call or write Lucy del Priore, Publicity Coordinator, Puffin Books, 375 Hudson Street, New York, NY 10014-3657; (212) 366-2819; fax: (212) 366-2012.

Puffin also offers the *Puffin Papers* newsletter. It is available free, three times a year, and includes a listing called "Free Stuff" for teachers.

RANDOM HOUSE
201 East 50th Street
New York, NY 10022
(212) 572-2600; fax: (212) 572-4960

Ask for: Catalog and promotional materials for your age group. Random House publishes books for children from preschool age through elementary school.

Requirements: No particular requirements listed. Send postcard or mail request on school letterhead when possible.

RIZZOLI INTERNATIONAL PUBLICATIONS, INC.
300 Park Avenue South
New York, NY 10010
(212) 387-3400; fax: (212) 387-3535

Ask for: Catalog and promotional materials for your age group. (These books are geared for readers from grade three through young adult.) List includes fiction and nonfiction, picture books, and story books that introduce children to multicultural themes and the fine arts.

Requirements: No particular requirements listed. Send postcard or mail request on school letterhead when possible.

SCHOLASTIC INC.
Attn: Rosalie Vitale
555 Broadway
New York, NY 10012-3999
(212) 343-6100; fax: (212) 343-4949

Ask for: Posters, teaching guides, classroom activity guides to First Discovery Books, and current brochure featuring Scholastic's multicultural titles. Imprints include:

- Blue Ribbon: classic picture book reprints
- Little Apple: for readers 7–9
- Apple Paperbacks: 8–13
- Point Books: 12 and up

Scholastic has also developed:

- Core Instructional Programs
- Reading Technology
- Literature-based Programs
- CD-ROM Motivating Technology
- Scholastic Math Place
- Science Place
- Spanish Language Products and Programs

Call (800) 325-6149 to ask questions, receive further information, and to order catalogs.

Requirements: Self-addressed label with 9-oz. first-class postage.

SIERRA CLUB BOOKS
85 Second Street
San Francisco, CA 94105
(415) 977-5734; fax: (415) 977-5792

Ask for: Catalog and promotional materials for your age group. Books center on environmental and nature themes. Picture books, novelty projects, and middle-grade nonfiction are available.

Requirements: No particular requirements listed. Send postcard or mail request on school letterhead when possible.

SIMON AND SCHUSTER JUVENILE PUBLICATIONS
866 3rd Avenue
New York, NY 10022
(212) 698-7200

Ask for: Packet containing five postcards each of two current feature titles, 10 bookmarks, a poster.

Requirements: 10″ × 13″ SASE with 5-oz. first-class postage.

STEMMER HOUSE PUBLISHERS, INC.
Attn: CBC Offer
2627 Caves Road
Owings Mills, MD 21117
(410) 363-3690

Ask for: Posters for current books.

Requirements: 10″ × 13″ SASE with 7-oz. first-class postage.

TAMBOURINE BOOKS
Attn: CBMD
1350 Avenue of the Americas
New York, NY 10019
(212) 261-6500

Ask for: Poster of *The Joke's on George.*

Requirements: Self-addressed label with 3-oz. first-class postage.

THOMSON LEARNING, INC.
One Pennsylvania
New York, NY 10001

Ask for: Catalog and promotional materials for your age group. Books are aimed at students K–9. Gives you the chance to extend textbook learning and enhance curriculum by providing books that are appropriate for more than one grade on topics that span the curriculum, books that encourage a creative approach to teaching by introducing various approaches to a topic, and books with hands-on activity projects included within. Also has a D&D program wherein some defective books are available for a limited time.

Requirements: 10″ × 12″ SASE required to receive posters (four currently available). Pens, pads, and stickers available for a limited time—send business SASE for these. Also has free curriculum guide for teachers, available for SASE. Note: SASE postage depends upon what you wish to order. You will need $1.00 of postage minimum. If you want all of the posters, or one of everything, add $3.00 postage.

TINY THOUGHT PRESS
1427 South Jackson Street
Louisville, KY 40208-2720
(800) 456-3208; fax: (502) 634-1693

Ask for: Catalog and promotional materials for your age group. The Tiny Thought Books are aimed at students K–6 and are stories with character-building messages featuring the character Littlest Tall Fellow. The full-color books are 32 pages long.

Requirements: No particular requirements listed. Send postcard or mail request on school letterhead when possible.

VIKING
Penguin USA
375 Hudson Street
New York, NY 10014
(212) 366-2000

Ask for: Catalog and promotional materials for your age group. Publishes a list that includes preschool through young adult. List includes picture books, pop-ups, novelty books, board, toddler, fiction, and nonfiction. Series titles include:

- Women of Our Time
- Once upon America

Requirements: No particular requirements listed. Send postcard or mail request on school letterhead when possible.

WALKER PUBLISHING COMPANY
435 Hudson Street
New York, NY 10014
(212) 727-8300; fax: (212) 727-0984

Ask for: Catalog and promotional materials for your age group. Also has a small D&D program. Ask for information about it.

Requirements: No particular requirements listed. Send postcard or mail request on school letterhead when possible.

WILLIAM MORROW JUNIOR BOOKS

Attn: Lori Benton
Division of William Morrow & Company, Inc.
1350 Avenue of the Americas
New York, NY 10019
(212) 261-6792; fax: (212) 261-6785;
website: www.williammorrow.com

Ask for: Catalog and promotional materials for your age group. Has many postcards, posters, and biographical materials available, but as these are promotional items, no one poster or postcard will be available at all times. Produces approximately six new posters and five new postcards per season (spring and fall). Teachers' guides featuring tips and activities are available.

Requirements: All materials are free, but each request should be accompanied by $1.50 in postage.

WORKMAN PUBLISHING COMPANY

Attn: Publicity
708 Broadway
New York, NY 10003
(212) 254-5900; fax: (212) 475-5074

■ One of the great children's book publishers, and you can obtain their catalog for free. In it, you will find reasonably priced books and games (including the famous *Brain Quest*® and *The Bones and Skeleton Gamebook*). A truly neat resource for teachers, kids, and parents alike.

Ask for: Catalog. Also, upon request, offers a special teacher's and/or parents' guide for the following titles:

• *Brain Quest*® Grades 1–7: teacher's and parents' guide
• *Brain Quest*® Preschool and Kindergarten: parents' guide*
• *Brain Quest*® *for Threes* (ages 3–4): parents' guide*
• *My First Brain Quest*® (ages 2–3): parents' guide*
• *Do People Grow on Family Trees?* by Ira Wolfman

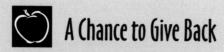

A Chance to Give Back

In a program called "Book Angel," books purchased are donated to help seriously ill children experience the pleasure of good reading. If your students get involved, the books you donate will feature bookplates listing your class or school. This is a holiday program—your books will even be gift-wrapped. For further information, call Anderson's Books at (630) 355-2665.

• *The Kids' Book of Questions* by Gregory Stock, Ph.D.

* These parents' guides are perfectly suitable for teachers' use.

Requirements: None.

Magazine Publishers

STONE SOUP, THE MAGAZINE BY YOUNG WRITERS AND ARTISTS
P.O. Box 83
Santa Cruz, CA 95063-0083
(800) 447-4569; fax: (408) 426-1161;
website: www.stonesoup.com

■ *Ms.* magazine calls *Stone Soup* "*The New Yorker* of the 8 to 13 set." Published by the Children's Art Foundation (located in Santa Cruz, California), it is devoted entirely to the writing and art of children. The magazine is well designed and stylish. Author photos grace the stories and poems, reminding young readers that the magazine's content was produced by peers . . . thus encouraging their own reading and writing.

Subscribing to *Stone Soup* is an excellent introduction to its parent organization, the Children's Art Foundation, which also publishes books illustrated and written by children, and reproduces art from the Museum of Children's Art onto postcards. More than a reading-writing tool for teaching, it is an outstanding format to remind children (and adults as well) that children's culture has a voice and viewpoint. Additionally, every issue includes an activities section with ideas that can be used at home or as the basis for classroom assignments to get children involved in writing and art.

Ask for: Brochure.

Requirements: Toll-free number above will provide ordering information.

CHILDREN'S SURPRISES MAGAZINE, ACTIVITIES FOR TODAY'S KIDS AND PARENTS
1200 N. 7th Street
Minneapolis, MN 55411
(800) 356-8899; fax: (612) 522-1182

■ *Children's Surprises Magazine, Activities for Today's Kids and Parents* is an exciting, color graphics magazine for children 5–12. It offers educational projects that can be used for sponge activities or for student enjoyment. Published bimonthly: $14.95/year (six issues). Teacher subscription discount price is $8.95/year (order on school letterhead).

Ask for: Sample copy.

Requirements: Send $2.00 to cover shipping and handling.

WHO CARES
1511 K Street, NW, Suite 1042
Washington, DC 20005
(202) 628-1691

■ Some young journalists, countering the "no one cares" attitude usually attributed to members of "Generation X," have founded a national magazine called *Who Cares, A Journal of Service and Action.* This new quarterly journal features inspiring stories of young volunteers, entrepreneurs, and activists. Each issue includes a directory of national and community-oriented service organizations.

Ask for: Ordering information.

Requirements: Published quarterly; $15.00/year for individuals, $20.00/year for organizations.

Other Organizations and Programs

ALA GRAPHICS
The American Library Association (ALA)
50 East Huron Street
Chicago, IL 60611
(800) 545-2433, press 8

■ ALA is an organization that promotes reading and literacy. Its ALA Graphics catalog is free for the asking. In addition to posters and bookmarks, it features reading promotion materials, and lists of Caldecott and Newberry medal books.

Ask for: ALA Graphics Catalog.

Requirements: Send postcard or letter with your name and address.

BOOK IT!
P.O. Box 2999
Wichita, KS 67201
(800) 4-BOOK IT; fax: (316) 687-8937

■ Book It! is a free reading incentive program created by Pizza Hut. The five-month program is for children in grades K–6. Book It! is guided by the teacher who sets monthly reading goals for each child in the classroom. When that monthly reading goal is met, the child is presented with a Pizza Award Certificate, redeemable at participating Pizza Hut restaurants.

Pizza Hut points out clearly that "All Book It! materials and awards are free of cost. No purchase is required at the restaurant, and the pizza can be taken to go." At Pizza Hut, the child receives personal congratulations by the manager, a free one-topping Personal Pan Pizza, and a button with a 3-D sticker. The child will receive another pizza and sticker each month that the reading goal is met. If the reading goal is met all five months, the student qualifies for the Reader's Honor Roll for classroom student achievement.

Pizza Hut will give children and teachers a free classroom pizza party if the reading goals are met by all the children in any four of the five program months. Book It! is the only reading incentive program you will need, and it will fit into the rest of your reading program easily . . . it could become a "spine" of motivation.

Ask for: Free booklets on: program descriptions, program instructions, parent letters, parent verification form, honor roll poster, large multicolor reading progress chart, and a resource pamphlet for program enhancement that includes inexpensive incentive items (T-shirts, stickers, certificates of achievement, book report folders, magic sport bags).

Book It! also publishes a booklet of ideas on enhancing the program, written by teachers who have used it. To obtain a copy of this free booklet (and ideas on celebrating National Young Reader's Day) call the toll free number above and order #62959. Book It! has also reprinted a Department of Education brochure titled Help Your Child Become a Good Reader. (Suggest this to parents.) Write or call for a free copy. Order #62960.

Requirements: None.

CALIFORNIA DEPARTMENT OF EDUCATION
P.O. Box 271
Sacramento, CA 95812-0271
(916) 657-2451; fax: (916) 657-4975

■ A leader in education and curriculum development, the Department offers more than 500 publications and videotapes to educators and other interested citizens at cost. Shipping is included, and only California residents pay the state sales tax. The catalog

Poster for Banned Books Week

Teach the importance of our freedom to read! New Banned Books Week kit each year. Available in June, for Banned Books Week in fall. Contact the American Library Association. Posters are $5.00 each plus shipping and handling. Call (800) 545-2433, ext. 4220.

is available at no cost and lists curriculum frameworks, curriculum guides, and handbooks (all prices include shipping and only California residents pay state sales tax). The California Department of Education is a leader in producing education documents, one of which has become a model for national elementary education advancement.

Ask for: Publications catalog.

Requirements: None.

THE CHILDREN'S BOOK COMMITTEE (CBC)
Bank Street College of Education
610 West 112th Street
New York, NY 10025
(212) 875-4540; fax: (212) 875-4759

■ CBC is a valuable resource because it could so easily fit under several categories. CBC serves teachers, parents, librarians, *and* students (as well as *any* readers interested in children's literature). They assist in identifying the best children's books of the year, offering carefully prepared and up-to-date information. The nonprofit CBC has been operating for 75 years, publishing widely acclaimed lists of books for children from infancy to age 14. The CBC is comprised of educators, authors, parents, librarians, psychologists, illustrators, and specialists in various fields. They are guided by the following criteria for fiction:

- quality and age-suitability of text and illustrations
- credibility of character and plot
- authenticity of time and place
- positive treatment of ethnic and religious differences
- absence of sexist stereotypes

And for nonfiction:

- accuracy
- clarity
- readability
- careful differentiation of fact from theory and opinion
- emotional and ethical impact on young readers

They also publish:

- *Children's Books of the Year*, 1998 Edition: $8.00 (plus $1.25 for postage)
- *Children's Books of the Year*: (previous years), $3.00
- *Books to Read Aloud with Children of All Ages*: $5.00

Ask for: Information on the CBC or directly order the titles above.

Requirements: For information, none. For orders, the CBC asks that you include payment as they are a nonprofit service.

THE CHILDREN'S LITERATURE CENTER

Library of Congress
First Street and Independence Avenue SE
Washington, DC 20540
(202) 707-5535

Ask for: Recommended children's books.

Requirements: None.

GREAT BOOKS FOUNDATION

35 East Wacker Drive, Suite 2300
Chicago, IL 60601
(800) 222-5870; fax: (312) 407-0334

■ The Junior Great Books program is geared for grades K–12 to help students become top readers.

Ask for: Free Junior Great Books information.

Requirements: None.

INTERNATIONAL READING ASSOCIATION (IRA)

800 Barksdale Road
P.O. Box 8139
Newark, DE 19714-8139
(302) 731-1600 or (800) 336-READ; fax: (302) 731-1057;
website: www.reading.org

■ IRA, "the largest professional organization worldwide dedicated exclusively to reading instruction," is a vast and varied resource. Programs ranging from free brochures to full-scale membership help keep you at the top of your field.

Ask for: Membership information. Various annual memberships from $30.00 to $95.00. IRA publishes books, four journals, a newspaper, and provides substantial savings from the IRA Book Club. As a member you will also have access to networking opportunities, conventions and conferences, council involvement, special interest groups, voting privileges, association advocacy, an award program, and many money-saving benefits. Brochures include:

- "Common Ground"—fighting censorship, protecting the human right to freedom of opinion
- "Family Literacy"—why it is important; what is being done; organizations for further information
- List of parent brochures for encouraging young people to read and ways that parents can help their children's educational development.

Single copies of parent brochures available upon request. Send SASE (business-size) with the appropriate postage attached: 1–3 titles—one first-class stamp; 4–7 titles—two first-class stamps; 8–12 titles—three first-class stamps.
Book lists include:

- Children's choices—list of favorite books of elementary school students
- Young adults' choices—favorite books of junior and senior high school students
- Teachers' choices

Single copies of each list are $1.00 in U.S. currency. Mail to Dept. EG at above address. Bulk quantities are available at the following prices (listed in U.S. currency): 10 copies—$5.00; 100 copies—$40.00; 500 copies—$150.00.

All orders must be prepaid and check must be made payable to IRA. A free catalog of publications is available, and you can write to the IRA for information on Newspaper in Education Week. (See box.)

Requirements: Listed above, with description offer.

KIDSNET
6856 Eastern Avenue, NW, Suite 208
Washington, DC 20012

■ The national clearinghouse for information on electronic media such as children's cable, television, radio, audio, and video.

Ask for: Free KIDSNET handbook.

Requirements: None.

Newspaper in Education Week

Participate in Newspaper in Education Week! This program encourages the use of newspapers in teaching by bringing daily newspapers into the classroom to help teach subjects ranging from social studies and reading to science and geography. It is cosponsored by the International Reading Association (IRA), the Newspaper Association of America Foundation, and the National Council for the Social Studies. The project usually takes place the first week in March, and aims to make lifelong newspaper readers of students.

Newspaper in Education (NIE) Week teaches that:

- Everyone can become better informed by reading newspapers.
- Newspapers reinforce the skills taught across the curriculum at all levels.
- Newspapers update the facts found in textbooks; they are a source of immediate news and have more in-depth analysis than television reports. They can be considered, if you will, instant textbooks.
- Reading newspapers is enjoyable as well as educational.
- Fun reading helps motivate learning.
- Newspapers help teachers explore new teaching approaches and resources.

But children need models—teachers and parents—to use newspapers and show their importance. The newspaper industry and the associations cosponsoring NIE Week know the importance of starting children on learning, thinking, and acting upon the world around them . . . starting with the practice of reading newspapers daily.

> The NIE program is a merger of local schools and local newspapers (more than 700 newspapers across Canada and the United States sponsor NIE programs). For more information, call your local newspaper and ask about NIE Week. (For the *New York Times*'s NIE program, call 800-631-1222.)

MCCRACKEN EDUCATIONAL SERVICES, U.S.A., INC.

United States Warehouse
4300 Sweet Road
Blaine, WA 98230
(800) 447-1462

■ The McCrackens are a Canadian-based teaching team, as well as sought-after speakers and workshop leaders. Their educational services methods emphasize language skills for beginning reading, writing, and spelling. Materials include books, pocket word chart and picture cards, themes, song tapes, professional texts, and videos.

Ask for: Catalog.

Requirements: No particular requirements listed. Send postcard or mail request on school letterhead when possible.

NATIONAL COUNCIL OF TEACHERS OF ENGLISH (NCTE)

Membership Service Representative
1111 West Kenyon Road
Urbana, IL 61801-1096

■ NCTE publishes materials on reading and literature for teachers, parents, and students in an effort to help children become fully developed readers.

Ask for: NCTE catalog.

Requirements: None.

NEWSPAPER ASSOCIATION OF AMERICA FOUNDATION

Attn: Toni F. Laws, Senior Vice President
1921 Gallows Road, Suite 600
Vienna, VA 22182
(703) 902-1600; fax: (703) 902-1736; www.naa.org

Ask for: Information about NIE programs.

Requirements: None.

NATIONAL LIBRARY SERVICE FOR THE BLIND AND PHYSICALLY HANDICAPPED (NLS)

The Library of Congress
Washington, DC 20542
(800) 424-8567; (202) 707-5100; fax: (202) 707-0712

■ Children who have physical or visual disabilities can learn to obtain the benefits of reading through the Library of Congress's NLS program. Braille books and recorded books and magazines (as well as special record and cassette players) are loaned and shipped postage-free to eligible persons.

In addition, NLS has information (in print) about physical and visual disabilities. These resources have particular benefit to teachers and parents who wish to learn more about the blind and physically handicapped. These materials can help you teach, help a disabled student to learn, help parents, and help teach all students an invaluable lesson in understanding others. Even if you do not have (or anticipate) a blind or physically handicapped student, you could use the materials—free braille alphabet cards, bookmarks, and fact sheets—to create lessons on disability awareness, the five senses, or the facts of blindness.

Ask for: General information on NLS and alphabet cards for your classroom.

Requirements: No particular requirements for the above materials. Send postcard or mail request on school letterhead when possible.

READING IS FUNDAMENTAL, INC. (RIF)

Publications Department
600 Maryland Avenue SW, Suite 600
Washington, DC 20024
(202) 287-3220; fax: (202) 287-3196; website: www.si.edu/rif

■ RIF is a nonprofit organization whose goal is to help young people acquire lifelong reading skills. RIF works toward national literacy by getting books to kids, motivating young readers, and encouraging parental participation in children's development as readers.

Ask for: List of RIF publications for parents, or information on starting a RIF program in your school.

Requirements: None.

U.S. DEPARTMENT OF EDUCATION

Department 617Z
Consumer Information Center
Pueblo, CO 81009

Ask for: Helping Your Child Learn to Read, a parental participation booklet.

Requirements: Single copies free.

U.S. GOVERNMENT BOOKS

Publications for sale by the Government Printing Office
Superintendent of Documents
P.O. Box 371954
Pittsburgh, PA 15250-7954
(202) 783-3238 (8 A.M.–4 P.M. EST)

■ Uncle Sam publishes more than 15,000 books, periodicals, posters, pamphlets, and subscription services. Request a catalog to "window shop" for your many interests. An excellent way to obtain current and timeless information on . . . everything, including such topics as: health, impact reports, job search guides, environmental science/energy, education/family, geography/travel, business, vital records, defense, military history, maps, and international topics.

These publications are excellent teaching guides or overview material for your own teacher education. Likewise, the seemingly endless information is a great referral source for parent education.

Ask for: Catalogs.

Requirements: No particular requirements listed. Send postcard or mail request on school letterhead when possible.

Raising Self-Esteem via Reading and Doing

Great Books for Girls: More than 600 Books to Inspire Today's Girls and Tomorrow's Women. Kathleen Oden. New York: Ballantine, 1977.

This book includes descriptions of more than 600 children's books with strong female characters for readers ages two through fourteen. Author Oden explains, "Society teaches girls that females are valued for looking good and pleasing others. The media bombards us with unrealistic standards of beauty that drive adolescent girls to eating disorders, depression, and low self-esteem. At the same time, girls are pressured to focus on others' needs and lose track of their own needs. Girls have to develop interests and hobbies that don't depend on the approval of others. Trying new tasks, persisting in the face of setbacks, and mastering new skills are vital elements in building self-confidence.

"The books I describe will give girls models of females who are brave, capable, and intelligent, rather than beautiful and focused on relationships. I believe these are images girls need to offset those images in the media."

Additional titles that focus on building self-esteem include:

• *Everyday Blessings: The Inner Work of Mindful Parenting.* Myla and Jon Kabat-Zinn. New York: Hyperion, 1997. Highly recommended by major minds in the field, including Dr. Spock.

- *The Girl's Guide to Life: How to Take Charge of the Issues That Affect You.* Catherine Dee. Boston: Little, Brown, 1997.
- *How to Read Aloud to Kids.* Patrick Fraley. Auburn, Calif.: The Audio Partners Publishing Corp., 1994.
- *The Intentional Family: How to Build Family Ties in Our Modern World.* William J. Doherty, Ph.D. Reading, Mass.: Addison-Wesley, 1997. Mary Piper, author of *Reviving Ophelia*, says "Unlike many other writers who focus on pathology, Doherty points families toward practical ways to be stronger."
- *Living on Planet Parenthood.* Jeanne Elium and Don Elium. Berkeley, Calif.: Ten Speed Press/Celestial Arts Publishing, 1997.
- *Making Things: The Handbook of Creative Discovery.* Ann Sayre Wiseman. Boston: Little, Brown, 1997. Teaches children about the creative process (vision, planning, proceeding in work with a logical and orderly method). Highly recommended.
- *Nurture by Nature: Understand Your Child's Personality—and Become a Better Parent.* Paul D. Tieger and Barbara Barron Tieger. Boston: Little, Brown, 1997.
- *One Nation Indivisible: How Ethnic Diversity Threatens America.* J. Harvie Wilinson, III. Reading, Mass.: Addison-Wesley, 1997. The author sums up the thesis of this book: "New America requires new thinking on civil rights. Policies that were viable in the bipolar world of black and white will no longer work in a multicultural setting."
- *Parents and the Awakening of a Healthy Woman.* Jeanne Elium and Don Elium. Berkeley, Calif.: Ten Speed Press/Celestial Arts Publishing, 1994.
- *Parents and the Making of a Healthy Man.* Jeanne Elium and Don Elium. Berkeley, Calif.: Ten Speed Press/Celestial Arts Publishing, 1996.
- *Talk To Me: Stories and a Novella.* Carol Dines. New York: Delacorte Press, 1997. Fiction that explores feelings about love, morality, and relationships, recommended for teens.

- *The Vulnerable Child: What Really Hurts America's Children and What We Can Do About It.* Richard Weissbourd. Reading, Mass.: Addison-Wesley, 1996.

Better World Zine

One of the earliest and greatest electronic magazines is the *Better World Zine,* (http://www.betterworld.com/BWZ/backiss.htm), masterminded by Microsoft writer and top consultant Christopher K. Nelder. The *BW* Links Directory was graciously provided by, and reprinted from, Chris Nelder on behalf of *BWZ.* The Directory has everything from daily eco-news to where to subscribe to the best newsletters and discussion groups to a comprehensive Web directory and the *BW* search engine. If you're a *BW* kind of business or website you can even add your own link—free! You can find the *Better World* Links Directory at http://betterworld.com/BW/links/index.htm.

Chapter Three

Writing

"Books make us work, movies do all the work for us. However, one of the greatest achievements for a writer is when he has told his story so well that someone on the bus misses their stop because they are so engrossed in what is going on. In a movie theater, there is nothing to divert our attention. On that bus, there is the world moving on at its furious pace everywhere around us. To so completely capture the reader's attention in those surroundings is a feat close to real magic."

— JONATHAN CARROLL

 The six-word lesson for learning to write is "Read, read, read; write, write, write." The importance of the listings and activities in this chapter is simple: students derive more meaning and make more personal connections with the text when they follow a reading with a discussion of the material or a writing activity. The materials and activities listed here are geared to transform writing from an assignment to an activity wherein students communicate personal experience, express creativity, or relate concepts.

The writing process is inexorably linked to the thinking process; writing refines one's thinking, while cognitive activity produces deeper and more fluid writing. Improve your students' writing and you'll help them achieve deeper and deeper levels of thinking.

Writing Activities

Why are we listing writing activities? The answer is simple. As a teacher you know that 75 percent of your work is setting up lesson plans. So, just as you need to find deals to save money on expenses in the classroom, it also helps to have ideas on how to use the materials and deals you obtain. Writing activities can be used across the curriculum, which makes them particularly attractive and useful.

Create a Newspaper

Students can create newspaper reports of events in history as if they were daily news happening at that time. (Please, no tabloid headlines.) This activity can be an excellent method not only to learn writing, but also to learn about the past lifestyles. What was the economy like? Entertainment? Sports? Dip the paper in coffee and let it dry to create an aged, yellowed effect. It is then ready for display in an exhibit on a historical period.

Report a Contemporary News Event

Have students research an ongoing story from several different sources (*Newsweek*, daily newspaper, television) and report the story as if they were reporters writing for a daily newspaper. As an additional activity, study the coverage of a popular story in several different mediums. Does *Hard Copy* report the story in the same way as *Time* magazine? How is it different? Have students perform a news report as Ted Koppel might and as an MTV reporter would. When is it all right to target a specific audience, drawing out certain facts for that audience? When is it tampering with the facts by altering perspective?

The Writing Process

Remember the concept of writing as a process, which breaks into simple yet consistent stages: prewriting, writing, sharing and responding, rewriting, editing, and evaluating. Turn the teaching of the writing process into a fun activity.

1. Select a writing topic for the students.

2. Do a prewriting activity, such as brainstorming, with the students. Other activities include motivation techniques such as playing inspirational music (related to the subject), taking a walk or going on a field trip in a related area (in a forest, by the sea, or through a historical setting), or using guided imagery to help students visualize and thus internalize various moods, times, and settings.

3. Write a "sloppy copy" draft. It is important to teach the students the difference between sloppy copy—which is word association (for the purposes of brainstorming)—and a "first draft." Many people feel writers should never think about a first draft, for drafts can be misunderstood as a wishy-washy concept that gives students the idea "they don't really have to try hard this time." Teach students to write as well as they can each and every time they write.

4. Have students share their work with the class or a select group and listen to the response. Then have the students rethink their paper. Try to schedule time (up to 24 hours) between looking at the work, to gain some distance from the writing.

5. Conduct an "editor" meeting with your students on an individual basis. You give them feedback from your point of view (adult/teacher/editor). Help them to find a focus for their rewrite.

6. Have students rewrite their papers along the editorial lines you have suggested (incorporating appropriate student response). They then put together all the ideas into a clear vision. (This step can go through several cycles of revision and teacher response.)

7. Collect students' papers. (Some call this step publishing.") Correct this copy as final work.

Creative Writing

The frame of a story or novel is surprisingly simple. In starting a creative writing unit, continue with the writing process your students have been developing. Discuss a book you read in class or show a popular video and discuss its storyline. Go through brainstorming sessions in which students develop their own stories. (You may offer themes or a beginning sentence or a subject to help jump-start those who get stuck.)

Have students answer these questions:

1. Who is the main character (and secondary characters) in your story?
2. Where does the story take place?
3. When does the story take place?
4. What is the story about?
5. When does "the problem" begin? (Discuss the fundamental role of conflict in literature.)
6. How is the story ended? Is the problem solved? Is the ending a happy or sad one? (Discuss the importance of not writing convenient endings—the million dollar check that arrives and just happens to save the poor family.)

Postwriting

Postwriting is revising, editing, and proofreading. Make an activity of checking word usage, spelling, sentence completeness, and overall style. Postwriting teaches that mechanical correctness is important—and should be done after the writing process. Postwriting will free students' minds for context flow, allowing proper grammar to evolve into the early draft process. It teaches students to double-check, take pride in their work, and learn to "cross t's and dot i's" before turning in papers.

Write a Letter to an Author

Have students write a letter to the author of the book they have just read and mail it, care of the publisher. Ask them to discuss their feelings about the book and why it had an impact on them.

Later they can share with the class any response they receive from the author.

Write a Letter to the Editor

Get students to write letters to the editor of your local or major city newspaper concerning topics of interest. This activity is more than writing practice—it encourages students to read the newspapers more carefully, and provides an understanding that world issues involve them.

Write a Real Job Application

Do you have students who are considering an after-school job of some sort? (Depending on the grade level, jobs can range from selling mail-order products, newspaper routes, babysitting, or work at a restaurant.) Those serious about getting work should write their job applications or letters to the appropriate person at the companies where they are applying for work.

Write and Publish a Book

Students can write their own book and even publish it, especially in these days of desktop publishing. The ideas are endless: a history of their town, a pamphlet on an important school issue that also affects the community, a fund-raiser idea (favorite recipes, etc.). The book can then be sold at school or town functions or through various community organizations.

Write for the School Literary Magazine

Assign creative writing projects (essays, poems, stories) for potential publication in the school literary magazine.

Write to Politicians and Civic Organizations

Get your kids involved in social action. The politics and crises around them (local and global) do matter. What important issues are going on right now in your town? In the nation? In the world? Discuss the conflicts and students' feelings on the subjects. Then have them write to the powers that be in political and civic organizations.

Write to Friends and Grandparents

Teach students to write for an audience by asking them to tell the same story in a letter to a friend and then to a grandparent or other relative. How does the tone change in each letter? What ways do they tell the story differently to their friends? Their grandparents? Why do they choose certain details for each? Do they see the effect of a carefully selected, telling detail? Show them how to use greeting, body, and closing in all letters. (As a bonus, friends, grandparents, and relatives will enjoy hearing from them.)

Other Letters

Students can write real or fictional invitations, thank-you notes, congratulation cards, sympathy cards, and regret notes.

Enter Writing Contests

Many magazines and groups offer writing contests. Contests can be an excellent way to practice writing for an audience.

Learn About Other States

Write a letter to the editor of a newspaper in a selected city asking people of a certain state to send your class postcards or a letter describing their state. Having a "sister" state or class is a good way to begin a study of that state. Research the state's employment picture, resources, exports, etc.

Join Pen Pal Clubs

As listed in the following writing resources section of this chapter, pen pals can be an outstanding way to communicate with others, to expand one's knowledge of human nature and of the world, and to think globally.

Start an individual or classroom (class-to-class) penfriendship. Post a map in your classroom to keep track of where the penfriends are. Have students begin a scrapbook of letters and souvenirs they have exchanged.

A High-Tech Variation on the Pen Pal Club

Of course the Internet is the biggest high-tech variation on penfriends, but the video camera is another high-tech twist. In establishing a penfriendship with another class, you may expand your relationship into other dimensions. Instead of sending a letter, why not make a video of the entire class, each student telling about him or herself for one minute? Perhaps the classes could do an information exchange via video, or compare and contrast their states.

Writing Resources

CALIFORNIA DEPARTMENT OF EDUCATION
515 L Street, Suite 250
P.O. Box 271
Sacramento, CA 95812-0271
(916) 657-2451, (916) 323-0823, (800) 995-4099;
website: www.//goldmine.cde.ca.gov/publications/pub.html

■ The California Department of Education (a publications bureau not limited to serving Californians) has a good-value resource titled *Handbook for Planning an Effective Writing Program*. It covers the age gamut from grades K–12 and includes an important parent-education appendix: "How to Help Your Child Become a Better Writer." One of its most popular titles is *Practical Ideas for Teaching Writing as a Process*.

Ask for: The titles listed above.

Requirements: $8.00 per copy.

THE EXPLORATORIUM

3601 Lyon Street
San Francisco, CA 94123
(415) 563-7337, (415) 561-0393 (to order poster);
fax: (415) 353-0481

■ The Exploratorium, the museum of science in San Francisco, offers a 22" × 33" poster called *A Story of Letters*, which traces the evolution of each letter of the modern alphabet (from Phoenician, Hebrew, Greek, and Latin), as well as showing a history of writing systems from 1700 B.C. to the present. A teacher's supplement is included with the poster. A fascinating introduction to the rich world of letters and writing.

Ask for: *A Story of Letters* poster, item #12550000.

Requirements: $10.00 each plus $4.50 postage and handling. California residents add sales tax.

INTERNATIONAL PEN FRIENDS (IPF)

Attn: Connie Hicks
1308 68th Lane North
Brooklyn Center, MN 55430
(612) 566-9722

■ Becoming a pen pal, or starting a pen pal club at your school, is a great hands-on method for developing practical and informational writing skills that can be used across the curriculum. IPF is regarded as the oldest and largest penfriend organization in the world. IPF is open to the young and elderly alike, male and female, and has 300,000 members in 156 countries. Benefits include making new friends and being able to practice writing or a foreign language, sharing information on a variety of subjects, and exchanging various articles such as books or records.

IPF will ask potential pen pals which of the following subjects are of interest to them: art, animals, antiques, camping, chess, computer science, crafts, dancing, exchanging holidays, fishing, frank discussion, gardening, history, literature, languages, music, photography, religious discussion, reading, science, social work, sport, theater, travel, and writing. Article exchange includes cards, stamps, souvenirs, dolls, tapes, books, and records.

Ask for: Forms S100E/700.

Requirements: Information is free, but IPF has admission fees ($11.95 for one person under 15). The admission fees include a surcharge in order to provide free or subsidized memberships to members in countries who are suffering political oppression or economic distress. *Club Magazine* is also available for $9.00 for one issue or $26.00 for an annual subscription (four issues). A comprehensive program is available especially for teachers, classes, and groups serving youth aged 10–17 years.

JOHN GILE COMMUNICATIONS
1710 North Main Street
Rockford, Illinois 61103
(815) 968-6601; fax: (815) 968-6600

■ The story behind author John Gile's bestselling book, *The First Forest*, and his subsequent author-visit program is remarkable. Originally, the midwestern journalist was simply writing a story for his children on the importance of being kind to one another. The story was published and has since been used by teachers in language arts, graphic arts, whole language science, peace, and environmental issues, and school musical productions. Gile's school-visit program is called "How a Book Is Born." The program emphasizes the importance of reading and of students developing communication skills to further their own creativity, writing, and academic work.

Another Gile bestseller, *Oh, How I Wish I Could Read!* is also available on audiocassette. Illustrated by award-winning artist Frank Fiorello, this highly acclaimed bestseller is the perfect book for teachers who laugh with their students and use humor to teach. You can receive the cassette free with the book if you mention *Unbelievably Good Deals That You Absolutely Can't Get Unless You're a Teacher* when you order through the publisher's direct-order line—(800) 747-6601.

Teachings from a Reading and Writing Program

John Gile's *The First Forest* teaches ethical and honorable behavior toward people and the entire ecosystem. The book was so successful that he developed a reading and writing program, *How a Book Is Born*, as well as a video of the program. His description of the core of the program sums up the teaching of writing:

> In the core program, students see an illustration of the process of finding, capturing, and developing ideas, writing a story, developing art, merging the writing and art, and producing a finished product. I explain that writing even a short story such as *The First Forest* is a process that requires writing, rewriting, revising, editing, putting some new things in, and taking some old things out—in short, what all writing requires. To illustrate the point, I show the students a thick stack of papers involved in the writing of *The First Forest*. To graphically reinforce that point, I also show students how the art evolved from early doodles made while searching for illustration concepts through the early sketch stage and finally into the full color which appears in the book.
>
> In the process, I explain the challenge writers and artists face in overcoming initial inertia and emphasize the importance of taking that first step—getting started. Then I show them an early mock-up or dummy and explain how we put the text and illustrations together. I explain some of the hundreds of decisions made in the process and show them the final mock-up or dummy which was used as a guide for the actual printing preparation. Finally I show them what the first sheets off the printing press look like and explain the printing process, including the critical importance of proper alignment, the process

for reproducing the paintings, and the finishing process: cutting the large press sheets, folding, collating, stitching, trimming, and putting on the hard cover. Throughout the program I provide anecdotes to encourage and motivate the students in their own work. At the end of the program, I answer students' questions. For teachers, I add material on motivating students to write.

The fee for the program (a good value resource) is $800 plus travel and lodging. Schools in the same area can combine for the program. For further information, call (815) 968-6601.

The *How a Book Is Born* program is also a videocassette focused on motivating students to develop their reading and writing skills. In 1994, some of the proceeds of this program were used to reforest 322 acres in Yellowstone. As the program description notes, "With your video, your school also becomes a participant in a national reforestation project based on The First Forest. Ten trees will be planted in your school's name at the First Forest in Greater Yellowstone (with acknowledgment from the National Arbor Day Foundation honoring your participation), or you may choose to receive 10 trees to plant at your school. You also will receive a gift membership in the National Arbor Day Foundation, a subscription to the Foundation members' newsletter *Arbor Day*, the *Tree Book* (except in California and Arizona due to shipping restrictions on nursery products), and access to additional educational resources of the National Arbor Day Foundation and the publishers of *The First Forest*. The price of the video is $49.95 plus shipping." To order, call (800) 747-6601 or mail to JGC Communications, 1710 North Main Street, Rockford, IL 61103-4706.

Ask for: Free teaching unit for *The First Forest*, which has applications beyond teaching the book. This cross-cultural and cross-curriculum unit can be used to teach various themes (from ecology to kindness) and has been teacher tested in more than 12,000 classrooms.

Requirements: None.

MERLYN'S PEN
P.O. Box 1058
East Greenwich, RI 02818
(800) 247-2027; fax: (401) 885-5222;
website: www.merlyn'spen.com

■ Call for free samples of this annual magazine of student writing. Encourage your students to submit essays, stories, poems, cartoons, and photos for publication.

Ask for: Free sample.

Requirements: Grades 6–12. Must include grade you teach when writing or calling. Students requesting submission sheets should address their letters to P.O. Box 910.

MILLIKEN PUBLISHING COMPANY
1100 Research Boulevard
P.O. Box 21579
St. Louis, MO 63132-0579
(800) 325-4136, (800) 538-1319;
website: www.millikenpub.com

■ Order a free CD-ROM on Milliken's products. This great freebie includes a lot of information on their popular program, "The Writing Process."

Ask for: Writing sample CD.

Requirements: Submit request in writing on school letterhead.

THE NATIONAL ELEMENTARY SCHOOLS PRESS ASSOCIATION (NESPA)

Mark Levin, Director
NESPA
Carolina Day School
1345 Hendersonville Road
Asheville, NC 28803
(828) 274-0758, ext. 397; website: www.nespa.org

■ NESPA is an organization that offers a free list of ideas and organizational tips on how to start newspapers for grades 1–6. Membership includes a how-to book and a triennial newsletter.

Ask for: A *free* four-page list of things to write about in school papers, along with tips about how to get started.

Requirements: SASE with two stamps for free list; $35.00 registration fee for membership (send for free list first, to sample). Membership includes how-to book, biannual newsletter, and special surprises sent throughout the year.

Planning an Author Appearance

Farrar, Straus & Giroux will provide free tips on organizing an author appearance if you write for information on programs and availability. (They may ask for a small honorarium.) Write: Marketing Department, Books for Young Readers, Farrar, Straus and Giroux, 19 Union Square West, New York, NY 10003.

An author appearance can make literature a real-life adventure for children. Do any children's authors live in your region? (If you don't know, ask children's publishers, who often provide such information as part of their author promotion process. Also, ask your local bookseller, who may have some ideas.) Do you know if your favorite children's author is publishing a new book and going on a national book tour this year or next? Publicists suggest that you plan as early as possible for your author appearance, perhaps six months to a year ahead of time. There are many different types of author appearances, including bookstore appearances, workshops, conferences, and school visitations.

Chapter Four

Social Studies

The best way to teach Social Studies is via immersion techniques. Turn the classroom into what you are studying! If you are studying ancient civilizations, then the classroom should look like that civilization. Fill it with the books, pictures, artifacts, music, foliage, costumes, and foods that represent that place and time! Make the classroom look like a photograph of that civilization come to life. If a time traveler stepped into your newly created Philadelphia of 1776, could you fool him or her into thinking it was real? Bring ancient cities back into being. Be a great forger of ancient coins; burn incense and sing chants from the East; prepare a feast from a Hawaiian village.

Explore "being there" experiences. If you are studying U.S. Government, take a trip to your local state capital. Seeing things firsthand is a very exciting way to make a lesson a real learning experience.

Social Studies Activities*

The following activities are immersion techniques and use cooperative learning. They can be adjusted to study any aspect of

* The activities in this section were created and generously provided by Vivian Hamilton.

social studies, from ancient civilizations to U.S. History to European History, and on and on . . .

Topics in Social Studies

The following topics are excellent sources of material to study in any social studies units:

- food
- tools
- clothes
- jewelry
- cooking utensils
- house models
- ancient artifacts
- postcards
- maps
- animals
- flags
- topography
- journals
- toys
- art
- communicated ideas
- cities, towns, and houses
- holidays
- time of civilization
- religions
- dioramas
- sports
- gods

Visual Display Board Presentation

Have students create their own display boards and present the boards to the class. Boards are a fun way to do research. An added benefit is that students teach each other, (e.g., one group of students creates a visual display board on one state or country, another group creates a board on another state or country, etc.). Videotape the presentations.

Students should learn the following during their presentations:

1. Name of civilization (or whatever subject area is being studied)
2. Dates of civilization
3. Map of civilization
4. Tourist attractions or historical sites
5. Topography
6. Clothing

7. Cities/towns/houses

8. Food

Select a group of four students for each civilization that you are studying. Make sure the groups are balanced academically and behaviorally.

Procedure (given to students):

1. Using the list of topics for each project, agree on a division of labor.

2. Spend an adequate amount of time researching your information.

3. Bring a poster board to school or use butcher paper for the board.

4. After making the items for the board, arrange them carefully and glue them down.

5. Rehearse your presentation talks. Each person must participate orally.

6. A costume will make your presentation more interesting and authentic. (Remember, the presentation will be videotaped.)

7. Perform.

8. Evaluation will be completed by you and your teammates.

9. Write out what you learned in detail.

Legacy Ceremony

Students investigate what they feel would be a legacy in the civilization (or whatever area of history being studied) they choose. Through this fun investigative process the students learn about different artifacts and the different uses for them in that civilization. You will be thrilled with the interesting ideas the students explore.

Procedure:

1. Form a group of three or four students and select an ancient civilization.

2. Research the civilization and choose three to six items that represent the legacy of the civilization.

3. Research how the item was used.
4. Make a three-dimensional symbol of the item to be used in the ceremony, e.g., miniature wagon wheel for Mesopotamia.
5. Write the ceremony. Include:
   - topic card with dates (to place on tripod)
   - large map with defined civilization
   - information about the item and how it was used
   - a ritual that turns over the item to future generations (audience)
   - a closing ceremony
6. Consider these options for the ceremony:
   - background music
   - food
   - candles
   - flowers and petals
   - costumes
   - decorated lectern
   - background setting (art of civilization)
7. Rehearse.
8. Conduct dress rehearsal (with props).
9. Perform and have fun!

Working Display Board

Create a display board that changes throughout the year. The display board shows questions the students have about the civilization they are studying. The students investigate the answers. When the questions are answered they must exchange the old questions for new ones.

Procedure:

1. Select group of three or four students. Choose groups by country sign-up. No best friends. No same-sex group. Evaluate to make sure the group is balanced.
2. Web questions about civilization.

3. Have students gather materials for civilization at home, school library, public library, travel agency, or in the classroom.
4. Have group survey materials.
5. Decide what will go on the display board. There must be a working component, e.g., true or false facts, attractions, questions, and answers.
6. Decide on division of labor.
7. Set up a schedule.
8. Do research and gathering.
9. Rehearse oral presentation.
10. Make presentation.
11. Perform self- and peer-evaluation in three areas: participation, presentation, display board.

Create an Encyclopedia

Students will create an encyclopedia for the civilization they are studying. They must use every letter of the alphabet.
Procedure:
1. Each group of three or four students will make an encyclopedia for a civilization.
2. The encyclopedia must include a picture of the flag, flower, bird, and seal from the civilization being studied.
3. Each letter of the alphabet must stand for something that is related to the civilization. Each page should include a simple illustration that represents the letter topic.

Create a Commercial

Students create a commercial about the civilization they are studying. This is a fun way to investigate history!
Procedure:
1. The commercial should be three to five minutes in length. Each person should have a speaking part.
2. Break into small groups that are based on a civilization.

3. Survey and skim available material.

4. Brainstorm ideas and organization of your commercial.

5. Research.

6. Write a script.

7. Decide on speaking parts and props.

8. Rehearse.

9. Videotape and present to the class.

Time Box Project

Students create a Time Box that reflects the civilization being studied. From the list of topics (see above) the students create a fun piece of history. Begin by dividing the class into eight groups, one for each civilization. Balance the group by sex and temperament.

Procedure:

1. Each group will make a Time Box (cardboard is fine) that represents the culture. It should be decorated accordingly. Put items that relate to each topic (see list of topics) inside the Time Box.

2. Decide on a division of labor. Divide jobs evenly so you cover the topics. You may add any you wish.

3. Research and make the items.

4. Make and decorate the Time Box.

5. Prepare and rehearse the presentation. Each person will have a speaking part. Each item must be explained as to what it is and how it's used. Use background music for your presentation.

6. Perform a self- and a group-evaluation at the end of the project.

Social Studies Sources

You can begin a social studies unit many ways and find many free resources to help you get started. How about teaching a study of geography? How did the land contribute to the people's shaping or reshaping of history? This section provides a list of famous historical sites to write for free maps and booklets detailing sites and places of interest. Hands-on information is an outstanding way to bring history to life. And don't forget about the history of your own state—what areas near your community would make an enlightening field trip?

Social studies is about today, yesterday, and the future. The history of tomorrow is happening today.

AMERICAN BAR ASSOCIATION (ABA)

750 N. Lake Shore Drive
Chicago, IL 60611
(312) 988-5000; (312) 988-5732 (marketing);
fax: (312) 988-5494; website: www.abanet.org/publiced

■ ABA produces low-cost teacher activities packets, each on a "constitutional theme": justice, equality, power, or liberty.

Ask for: Catalog.

Requirements: $2.50 each. Shipping and handling charges: $2.00 for orders up to $9.99; $3.95 for orders $10.00–$29.99. Illinois residents include 8.75 percent tax.

AMERICAN FOREST AND PAPER ASSOCIATION

1111 19th Street, NW
Washington, DC 20036
(202) 463-2700, (202) 463-2785, (800) 244-3090;
website: www.asandpa.org

■ Offers a free package on the history and making of paper and the preservation of the environment. Receive a poster on the history of paper's introduction in America; a booklet on paper's history; pamphlets on recycling and environmental concerns; a fact card on paper recycling; and a brochure on protecting the environment.

Ask for: Posters and wall charts.
Requirements: None.

BLUESTOCKING PRESS

P.O. Box 1014
Placerville, CA 95667-1014
(530) 621-1123, (530) 642-9222, (800) 959-8586

■ Bluestocking Press's mission is to combine "timetables, historical documents, books, music, toys, [and] audiotapes, into a multifaceted approach to studying history." The publisher's goal is to provide children with materials that promote critical thinking and discussion. Publishes books (pre-K to adult) with themes on strong American values.

Ask for: Bluestocking Press catalog.

Requirements: None.

CENTER FOR RESEARCH AND DEVELOPMENT IN LAW-RELATED EDUCATION (CRADLE)

Attn: Julia P. Hardin, Executive Director
Wake Forest University School of Law
2714 Henning Drive
Winston-Salem, NC 27106-4502
fax: (910) 721-3353; E-mail: hardinjp@wfu.edu

■ Publishes the Warren E. Burger National Repository for Educational Materials on Citizenship and the Constitution. Order select materials (often for only one or two dollars), on topics ranging from censorship and the First Amendment to women and equality and speeches of U.S. presidents.

    Also of interest from CRADLE:

1. *LREnet—An Electronic Bulletin Board for Citizenship Educators.* Teachers can download this unique service of law-related education directly onto their own computers using LREnet. In addition, teachers can communicate with other teachers who are members of the network and participate in conferences on current issues.

2. *SPICE—Special Programs in Citizenship Education.* A series of intensive week-long institutes for teachers.

3. *Interactive Video on the Supreme Court and the Bill of Rights.*

CRADLE and ABC News codeveloped this interactive software for a new educational video program on the Supreme Court and the Bill of Rights.

Ask for: Free packet, which includes a catalog of lesson plans, and a pocket-sized publication of the U.S. Constitution and the Declaration of Independence.

Requirements: None.

THE DEPARTMENT OF THE TREASURY
Bureau of Engraving and Printing
15th and Pennsylvania Avenue NW
Washington, DC 20226
(202) 622-2000

■ A free packet from the Bureau of Engraving and Printing provides complete information on how the U.S. Government designs, prints, and manufactures currency, securities, and postage stamps. If you are planning a trip to the capital, be sure to ask for the *Tour Information* pamphlet. This packet includes information sheets on everything you've always wanted to know about money: the history of the motto "In God We Trust," the origin of the "$" sign, facts about the paper and ink used to print currency, facts about portraits and designs used on currency, fun facts about money, and much more.

Ask for: Information packet on printing money.

Requirements: None.

NATIONAL AFRICAN AMERICAN MUSEUM PROJECT
Smithsonian Institution
900 Jefferson Drive, SW
A&I 1130, MRC 431
Washington, DC 20560
(202) 357-4500

■ Offers *Orator*, a newsletter about African Americans. Packed with information, the newsletter helps teachers, students, and parents understand the importance of African American culture and history.

Ask for: *Orator* newsletter. State the number of samples you need for your classroom and ask to be placed on their mailing list.

Requirements: None.

NATIONAL COUNCIL FOR THE SOCIAL STUDIES
3501 Newark Street, NW
Washington, DC 20016
(202) 966-7840; fax: (202) 966-2061;
E-mail: msimpson@ncsf.org; website: www.ncsf.org

■ The National Council for the Social Studies is a co-sponsor of Newspapers in Education (NIE) week. Newspapers provide immediate and up-to-date coverage of the world's situations and crises as they happen. They can be used to cover an ongoing event and to show the multifaceted aspects of a story or situation. The all-important skills of reading, analyzing, and writing can be taught using a newspaper.

Ask for: Information about NIE programs.

Requirements: None.

NATIONAL WOMEN'S HISTORY PROJECT
Dept. P
7738 Bell Road
Windsor, CA 95492
(707) 838-6000

■ Publishes a 40-page booklet with illustrations and photographs on Latina women from the 1700s to the present with bilingual captions and biographical information. An excellent resource for Women's History Month (March) bulletin boards.

Ask for: *Las Mujeres: Mexican-American/Chicana Women.*

Requirements: $11.00 for *Las Mujeres*; $14.95 for the Mexican-American/Chicana photo display set.

OFFICE OF EDUCATIONAL PROGRAMS

National Museum of American Art
Smithsonian Institution
MRC 210
Washington, DC 20560
(202) 357-3095; fax: (202) 633-2829;
website: www.nmaa.si.edu

■ Get a free copy of the teaching guide "The West as America," for students grades 5–12. This guide offers an excellent and entertaining example of how American artists circa 1800 drew a "less than objective" history of the westward movement, thus creating the "Western" mythology.

Ask for: Free copy.

Requirements: Teachers of grades 5–12.

SILVA ORIENTEERING SERVICES, USA

P.O. Box 1604
Binghamton, New York 13902-1604
(607) 779-2264 or (800) 847-1460; fax: (607) 779-2293

■ Provides information and materials to help teach students map and compass reading. Some of the free material they offer includes:

• *Teaching Aids Catalog*
• *So You Want to Know About Orienteering* (for kids)
• *The Orienteering Planning Guide: How to Get Started*
• Plastic sample (nonmagnetic) compass

In addition, teachers always receive a 20 percent discount on products found in the *Teaching Aids Catalog*.

Ask for: Information Kit.

Requirements: None.

SMITHSONIAN INSTITUTION
Office of Elementary Education
Arts and Industries Building
Room 1163, MRC 402
Smithsonian Institution
Washington, DC 20560
(202) 357-1300

■ The *Resource Guide for Teachers* lists free or low-cost books, video- and audiotapes, and posters. The subjects covered range from language arts, science, the arts, social studies, and history. Includes listings on organizations, agencies, and museums that are resources for teachers.

Ask for: Smithsonian Resource Guide for Teachers.

Requirements: None.

UNITED INDIANS OF ALL TRIBES FOUNDATION
Attn: *Daybreak Star*
Indian Cultural Center
P.O. Box 99100
Discovery Park
Seattle, WA 98199
(206) 285-4425

■ Offers a free sample of *Daybreak Star*, a magazine celebrating Native American cultures. Each issue contains activities, puzzles, games, student contributions, a teacher guide, and background information.

Ask for: Free sample of *Daybreak Star*.

Requirements: Include a self-addressed, stamped envelope (SASE) with two first-class postage stamps.

U.S. DEPARTMENT OF JUSTICE
Federal Bureau of Investigation
Washington, DC 20535
(202) 324-3000

■ The FBI has published this booklet on the criminal justice system and its related information services. It will interest those studying aspects of government, laws, and the complex ways people interact with the law.

Ask for: Cooperation: The Backbone of Effective Law Enforcement.
Requirements: None.

U.S. GEOLOGICAL SURVEY
Earth Science Information Center
507 National Center
Reston, VA 22092
(703) 648-4000; fax: (703) 648-4250; website: www.usgs.gov

■ Offers a free packet called "What Do Maps Show?" designed to help your grade 4–8 students learn to read maps and to show what they can learn from maps. Included are three reproducible maps, a poster, and four activity sheets.

Ask for: Free packet about maps.
Requirements: Teachers of grades 4–8.

Geographical and Historical Sites

You can obtain information on all of the following landmarks, parks, monuments, and areas of historical or geographical importance by writing to the specific site and asking for "tourism packets" to be used in the classroom.

You will be pleasantly surprised by the quality and quantity of information you receive, and at how easily the information can be used for hands-on activities or to create lesson plans. You will be able to use the materials not only to teach history, but also for

Studying Other Cultures? Try These Resources!

- For a free catalog of maps, posters, and manipulatives on Antarctica: *Laughing Star Press*, 8725 Davis Road, Maineville, OH 45039; (513) 683-5682.
- The Australian Catalog Company will send you its free, full-color catalog packed with resource materials for your Australian unit. (800) 808-0938.
- For a free, color catalog with information for your American Indian, pilgrim, or pioneer units: M&M, P.O. Box 5951, Orange, CA 92613. Includes craft ideas.

various themes relevant to today (e.g., conflict, independence, women in history). Samples of the kits, while they may vary, include such materials as:

- Visitors' guide to sites, activities, and special events
- Calendar of events
- Landscape, trail, and National Historic Site maps
- Profiles on National Parks that include information on the year the park was established, highest peaks, lowest elevation, famous sites, temperature range, precipitation, flora, wildlife, geological features, rivers and lakes, and visitor use. (Helpful for student reports.)
- Overviews on states' histories and facts, including useful information such as state bird, tree, flag, flower, insect, mineral, animal, fish, motto, and history as well as the state's geography, population, government, and commerce, and information on its largest cities and famous people.

Alabama

ALABAMA BUREAU OF TOURISM AND TRAVEL
401 Adams Avenue, Suite 126
Montgomery, AL 36104
(800) ALABAMA; website: www.touralabama.org;
E-mail: info@touralabama.org

**GREATER BIRMINGHAM CONVENTION
AND VISITORS CENTER**
2200 Ninth Avenue North
Birmingham, AL 35203
(800) 458-8085

Alaska

ALASKA DIVISION OF TOURISM
P.O. Box 110801
Juneau, AK 99811-0801
(907) 465-2010; fax: (907) 465-2287;
website: www.state.ak.us.tourism or www.travelalaska.com

ANCHORAGE CONVENTION AND VISITORS BUREAU
1600 A Street, Suite 200
Anchorage, AK 99501
(907) 276-4118

Arizona

ARIZONA OFFICE OF TOURISM'S TRAVEL CENTER
2702 N. 3rd Street, Suite 4015
Phoenix, AZ 85004
(888) 520-3434; fax: (602) 240-5475;
website: www.arizonaguide.com

**PHOENIX AND VALLEY OF THE SUN
CONVENTION AND VISITORS BUREAU**
1 Arizona Plaza
400 East Van Buren, Suite 600
Phoenix, AZ 85004-2290
(602) 254-6500 or (602) 252-5588 (hotline);
fax: (602) 256-5290 or (602) 253-4415;
website: www.arizonaguide.com/phxcvb

MONTEZUMA CASTLE
Montezuma Castle National Monument
P.O. Box 219
Camp Verde, AZ 86322

SUNSET CRATER/WUPATKI NATIONAL MONUMENTS
Route 3, Box 149
Flagstaff, AZ 86004

Arkansas

TOURISM DIVISION
Arkansas Department of Parks and Tourism
One Capitol Mall
Little Rock, AR 72201
(800) NATURAL (US except AK, HI); fax: (501) 682-1364;
website: www.arkansas.com

GREATER LITTLE ROCK CHAMBER OF COMMERCE
101 S. Spring Street, Suite 100
Little Rock, AR 72201
(501) 374-4871; fax: (501) 374-6018;
website: www.littlerockchamber.com

California

CALIFORNIA OFFICE OF TOURISM
801 K Street, Suite 1600
Sacramento, CA 95814
(800) TO-CALIF; website: www.gocalif.ca.gov

LOS ANGELES CONVENTION AND VISITORS BUREAU
633 West Fifth Street, Suite 6000
Los Angeles, CA 90071
(800) 228-2452, (213) 689-8822; fax: (213) 624-9746;
website: www.latimes.com

■ For discount coupons for Los Angeles sites (Universal Studios, etc.), write to 685 S. Figueroa Street, Los Angeles, CA 90017.

SAN DIEGO CONVENTION AND VISITORS BUREAU
401 B Street, Suite 1400
San Diego, CA 92101
(800) 577-9283, (619) 232-3101, or (619) 236-1212;
E-mail: sdinfo@sandiego; website: www.sandiego.org

DEATH VALLEY
Death Valley National Monument
Death Valley, CA 92328
(619) 852-4524

■ Also provides information on desert life, nature, sand dunes, and borax.

Colorado

COLORADO TRAVEL AND TOURISM AUTHORITY
(800) 265-6723

■ Press 1 for the 1998 Colorado Official State Vacation Guide and Colorado state map. Press 2 for the Winter Ski Guide.

Connecticut

CONNECTICUT VACATION CENTER
Tourism Division
505 Hudson Street
Hartford, CT 06106
(800) CT-BOUND (except AK, HI)

Delaware

DELAWARE DEVELOPMENT OFFICE
99 Kings Highway
P.O. Box 1401
Dover, DE 19903
(800) 441-8846 (except AK, HI)

District of Columbia

**WASHINGTON D.C. CONVENTION AND
VISITORS ASSOCIATION**
1212 New York Avenue, NW, 6th Floor
Washington, DC 20005
(202) 789-7000

**FREDERICK DOUGLASS MEMORIAL HOME
VISITOR'S CENTER**
P.O. Box 40060
Washington, DC 20066
(202) 426-5960

■ This African-American history bookshop can provide information for Black History Month, U.S History, or a theme on respect and liberty.

FREDERICK DOUGLASS NATIONAL HISTORIC SITE
1411 W Street, SE
Washington, DC 20020
(202) 426-5961

■ This site is dedicated to the legacy of one of the greatest American abolitionists, orators, and civil rights activists in our history.

THOMAS JEFFERSON MEMORIAL
c/o National Park Service
NCP-Central
900 Ohio Drive, SW
Washington, DC 20242
(202) 426-6822

VIETNAM VETERANS MEMORIAL
c/o National Park Service
NCP-Central
900 Ohio Drive, SW
Washington, DC 20242
(202) 485-9880

WASHINGTON MONUMENT
c/o National Park Service
NCP-Central
900 Ohio Drive, SW
Washington, DC 20242
(800) 505-5040

LINCOLN MEMORIAL
c/o National Park Service
NCP-Central
900 Ohio Drive, SW
Washington, DC 20242
(202) 426-6896

THE WHITE HOUSE VISITOR'S CENTER
National Capitol Region
National Park Service
President's Pike
Washington, DC 20242
(202) 208-1631; White House Tours: (202) 755-7798

Florida

FLORIDA DIVISION OF TOURISM SERVICES
Bureau of Visitor Services
107 West Gaines Street, Room 501D
Tallahassee, FL 32399-2000
(904) 487-1462

JACKSONVILLE CONVENTION AND VISITORS BUREAU
3 Independent Drive
Jacksonville, FL 32202
(800) 733-2668

**GREATER MIAMI CONVENTION AND
VISITORS BUREAU**
701 Brickell Avenue, Suite 2700
Miami, FL 33131
(800) 933-8448

Georgia

ATLANTA CONVENTION AND VISITOR'S BUREAU
233 Peachtree Street, Suite 2000
Atlanta, GA 30303
(404) 222-6688

GEORGIA DEPARTMENT OF INDUSTRY AND TRADE
Tourist Division
285 Peachtree Center Avenue, Suite 1000
Atlanta, GA 30303
(800) VISIT-GA

**MARTIN LUTHER KING, JR., NATIONAL
HISTORIC SITE**
526 Auburn Avenue, NE
Atlanta, GA 30312
(404) 331-3920

Hawaii

HAWAII VISITORS BUREAU
2270 Kalakaua Avenue
Honolulu, HI 96815
(808) 923-1811

Idaho

IDAHO DEPARTMENT OF COMMERCE
State House Mail
700 West State Street
Boise, ID 83720-2700
(800) 635-7820

NEZ PERCE
Nez Perce National Historic Park
P.O. Box 93
Spalding, ID 83551
(800) 615-8060

Illinois

DEPARTMENT OF COMMERCE AND COMMUNITY AFFAIRS
Information and Distribution Center
620 East Adams Street, Floor M1
Springfield, IL 62701
(800) 223-0121

ILLINOIS TOURIST INFORMATION CENTER
100 West Randolph Street, Suite 3–400
Chicago, IL 60601
(312) 744-2400

Indiana

TOURISM DEVELOPMENT
Department of Commerce
1 North Capitol, Suite 700
Indianapolis, IN 46204
(800) 759-9191

Iowa

DIVISION OF TOURISM
200 East Grand
Des Moines, IA 50309
(800) 345-IOWA (except AK, HI)

Kansas

KANSAS DEPARTMENT OF COMMERCE AND HOUSING
Travel and Tourism Development Division
Department of Commerce
700 SW Harrison, Suite 1300
Topeka, KS 66603-3712
(913) 296-2009 or (800) 2KANSAS

■ Teachers or students ordering a school packet should give two months' lead time.

Kentucky

TRAVEL
Department M.R.
P.O. Box 2011
Frankfort, KY 40602
(800) 225-TRIP, ext. 67

■ When teachers call or write, they will receive an *Official Vacation Guide*. When students call or write, they will receive a *Symbols and Traditions* brochure.

CONVENTION AND VISITORS BUREAU
400 South First Street
Louisville, KY 40202
(800) 626-5646

Louisiana

LOUISIANA OFFICE OF TOURISM
Inquiries Station
P.O. Box 94291
Baton Rouge, LA 70804-9291
(800) LA-ROUGE

GREATER NEW ORLEANS TOURISM AND CONVENTION COMMISSION
1520 Sugar Bowl Drive
New Orleans, LA 70112
(504) 566-5011

Maine

DEPARTMENT OF ECONOMIC AND COMMUNITY DEVELOPMENT
Office of Tourism
193 State Street
Augusta, ME 04333
(800) 533-9595 (except AK, HI)

Maryland

OFFICE OF TOURISM
Visitors Center
23 West Chesapeake
Towson, MD 21204
(800) 719-5900 (except AK, HI)

BALTIMORE AREA CONVENTION AND VISITORS CENTER
300 West Pratt Street
Baltimore, MD 21201
(800) 282-6632

THE STAR-SPANGLED BANNER FLAG HOUSE AND 1812 MUSEUM HISTORIC LANDMARK
844 East Pratt Street
Baltimore, MD 21202
(301) 837-1793

■ This historic landmark is the house of Mary Pickersgill, who sewed the flag that flew over Fort McHenry during the War of

1812 and inspired Francis Scott Key to write our national anthem. Adjacent museum commemorates the War of 1812 and has an audiovisual program.

Massachusetts

MASSACHUSETTS TRAVEL AND TOURISM
100 Cambridge Street, 13th Floor
Boston, MA 02202
(800) 447-MASS (except AK, HI)

**GREATER BOSTON CONVENTION
AND VISITORS BUREAU**
Prudential Tower
P.O. Box 490, Suite 400
Boston, MA 02199
(617) 536-4100

Michigan

MICHIGAN TRAVEL BUREAU
P.O. Box 30226
Lansing, MI 48909
(800) 5432-YES

**METROPOLITAN DETROIT CONVENTION
AND VISITORS BUREAU**
100 Renaissance Center, Suite 1950
Detroit, MI 48243-1056
(800) DETROIT

FLINT CONVENTION AND VISITORS BUREAU
Northbank Center, Suite 101-A
400 North Saginaw
Flint, MI 48502
(810) 232-8900

Minnesota

MINNESOTA OFFICE OF TOURISM
100 Metro Square Building
121 Seventh Place East
St. Paul, MN 55101
(800) 657-3700 (except AK, HI)

GREATER MINNEAPOLIS CONVENTION AND VISITORS ASSOCIATION
1219 Marquette Avenue South, Suite 300
Minneapolis, MN 55403
(612) 661-4700

ST. PAUL CONVENTION AND VISITORS BUREAU
101 Northwest Center
55 East Fifth Street
St. Paul, MN 55101-1713
(612) 297-6985

Mississippi

MISSISSIPPI DIVISION OF TOURISM
P.O. Box 849
Jackson, MS 39205-0849
(800) WARMEST

NATCHEZ CONVENTION BUREAU
P.O. Box 1485
Natchez, MS 39121
(601) 446-6345

Missouri

CONVENTION AND VISITORS BUREAU OF GREATER KANSAS CITY
City Center Square
1100 Main, Suite 2550
Kansas City, MO 64105
(800) 877-1234

CONVENTION AND VISITORS BUREAU OF GREATER ST. LOUIS
10 South Broadway, Suite 1000
St. Louis, MO 63102
(800) 888-3861

Montana

MONTANA DEPARTMENT OF COMMERCE
Travel Promotion
1424 Ninth Avenue
Helena, MT 59620
(800) VISIT-MT

CUSTER'S LAST STAND
Little Big Horn National Monument
P.O. Box 39
Crow Agency, MT 59022
(406) 638-2622

Nebraska

TRAVEL AND TOURISM DIVISION
301 Centennial Mall South
P.O. Box 94666
Lincoln, NE 68509
(800) 228-4307

Nevada

NEVADA COMMISSION OF TOURISM
5151 South Carson Street
Carson City, NV 89710
(800) NEVADA-8

LAS VEGAS CONVENTION AND VISITORS AUTHORITY
3150 South Paradise Road
Las Vegas, NV 89109
(702) 892-0711

New Hampshire

**DEPARTMENT OF RESOURCES AND
ECONOMIC DEVELOPMENT**
172 Pembroke Road
Concord, NH 03301
(800) FUN-IN-NH

New Jersey

NEW JERSEY DIVISION OF TOURISM
P.O. Box CN 826
Trenton, NJ 08625
(800) JERSEY-7

**ATLANTIC CITY CONVENTION AND
VISITORS BUREAU**
2301 Boardwalk
Atlantic City, NJ 08401
(609) 449-7130

EDISON NATIONAL HISTORIC SITE
Main Street and Lakeside Avenue
West Orange, NJ 07052
(973) 736-5050

New Mexico

NEW MEXICO DEPARTMENT OF TOURISM
Lamy Building
491 Old Santa Fe Trail
Santa Fe, NM 87503
(800) 545-2040

CARLSBAD CAVERNS
Carlsbad Caverns National Park
3225 National Parks Highway
Carlsbad, NM 88220
(505) 885-8884 or (505) 785-2232

New York

NEW YORK STATE DEPARTMENT OF ECONOMICS
Division of Tourism
1515 Broadway, 51st Floor
New York, NY 10036
(800) CALL-NYS

NEW YORK CONVENTION AND VISITOR BUREAU
Two Columbus Circle
New York, NY 11019
(213) 397-8222

North Carolina

NORTH CAROLINA DEPARTMENT OF COMMERCE
Travel and Tourism Division
430 North Salisbury Street
Raleigh, NC 27603
(800) VISIT-NC

CHARLOTTE CONVENTION AND VISITORS BUREAU
122 East Stonewall Street
Charlotte, NC 28202
(800) 231-4636

North Dakota

NORTH DAKOTA TRAVEL DEPARTMENT
Liberty Memorial Building
604 East Boulevard
Bismarck, ND 58505
(800) 435-5663

Ohio

OHIO OFFICE OF TRAVEL AND TOURISM
77 South High Street, 29th Floor
Columbus, OH 43266
(800) BUCKEYE (except AK, HI)

**GREATER CINCINNATI CONVENTION AND
VISITORS BUREAU**
300 West Sixth Street
Cincinnati, OH 45202
(800) 344-3445

Oklahoma

OKLAHOMA TOURISM AND RECREATION DEPARTMENT
2401 North Lincoln Boulevard, Suite 500
Oklahoma City, OK 73105-4492
(800) 652-6552 (except AK, HI)

NATIONAL COWBOY HALL OF FAME
1700 Northeast 63rd Street
Oklahoma City, OK 73111
(800) 225-5652

Oregon

OREGON TOURISM DIVISION
775 Summer Street, NE
Salem, OR 97310
(800) 547-7842

PORTLAND/OREGON VISITORS ASSOCIATION
26 SW Salmon Street
Portland, OR 97204-3299
(503) 222-2223

Pennsylvania

ALLENTOWN-LEHIGH COUNTY
Chamber of Commerce
462 Walnut Street
Allentown, PA 18102-5497
(800) VISIT-PA

PENNSYLVANIA DEPARTMENT OF COMMERCE
Bureau of Travel Development
453 Forum Building
Harrisburg, PA 17120
(717) 761-0702

PHILADELPHIA CONVENTION AND VISITORS BUREAU
1515 Market Street, Suite 2020
Philadelphia, PA 19102
(800) 225-5745

**GREATER PITTSBURGH CONVENTION
AND VISITORS BUREAU**
4 Gateway Center, Suite 514
Pittsburgh, PA 15222
(800) 366-0093

VALLEY FORGE
Valley Forge Convention and Visitors Bureau
P.O. Box 331
Norristown, PA 19404
(800) 441-3549

Rhode Island

**RHODE ISLAND DEPARTMENT OF
ECONOMIC DEVELOPMENT**
Tourist Promotion Division
Seven Jackson Walkway
Providence, RI 02903
(800) 556-2484

South Carolina

**SOUTH CAROLINA DEPARTMENT OF
PARKS, RECREATION, AND TOURISM**
Division of Tourism
1205 Pendleton Street
Columbia, SC 29201
(803) 734-0122

FORT SUMTER
Fort Sumter National Monument
1214 Middle Street
Sullivan's Island, SC 29482
(803) 883-3123

South Dakota

SOUTH DAKOTA DEPARTMENT OF TOURISM
711 East Wells Avenue
Pierre, SD 57501-3369
(800) SDAKOTA

MOUNT RUSHMORE NATIONAL MEMORIAL
P.O. Box 268
Keystone, SD 57751-0268
(800) 827-9323

Tennessee

TENNESSEE TOURIST DEVELOPMENT
P.O. Box 23170
Nashville, TN 37202
(615) 259-4730

KNOXVILLE CONVENTION AND VISITORS BUREAU
P.O. Box 15012
Knoxville, TN 37901
(423) 523-7263

MEMPHIS CONVENTION AND VISITORS BUREAU
45 Union Avenue
Memphis, TN 38103
(800) 873-6282

Texas

TEXAS DEPARTMENT OF COMMERCE
Tourism Division
P.O. Box 12728
Austin, TX 78711
(800) 452-9292 (except AK, HI)

DALLAS CONVENTION AND VISITORS BUREAU
1201 Elm Street, Suite 2000
Dallas, TX 75270
(214) 746-6677

FORT WORTH CONVENTION AND VISITORS BUREAU
415 Throckmorton Street
Fort Worth, TX 76102
(800) 433-5747

SAN ANTONIO MISSIONS
National Historical Park
2202 Roosevelt Avenue
San Antonio, TX 78210-4919
(800) 447-3372

Utah

UTAH TRAVEL COUNCIL
Council Hall, Capitol Hill
Salt Lake City, UT 84101-1493
(800) 200-1160

Vermont

VERMONT TRAVEL DIVISION
134 State Street
Montpelier, VT 05602
(800) VERMONT

Virginia

VIRGINIA DIVISION OF TOURISM
1021 East Cary
Richmond, VA 23219
(800) 932-5827

BOOKER T. WASHINGTON NATIONAL MONUMENT
Route 3, Box 310
Hardy, VA 24101
(540) 721-2094

NORFOLK CONVENTION AND VISITORS BUREAU
236 East Plume Street
Norfolk, VA 23510
(800) 368-3097

MONTICELLO
Virginia State Chamber of Commerce
9 South Fifth Street
Richmond, VA 23219
(800) 365-7272

MOUNT VERNON

Virginia State Chamber of Commerce
9 South Fifth Street
Richmond, VA 23219
(703) 780-2000

WILLIAMSBURG

Director of Media Relations
Colonial Williamsburg Foundation
P.O. Box 1776
Williamsburg, VA 23187
(800) 368-6511

JAMESTOWN-YORKTOWN FOUNDATION

P.O. Drawer JF
Williamsburg, VA 23187-3630
(757) 253-4838

■ The Jamestown-Yorktown Foundation is a nonprofit organization that administers two parks for the state of Virginia, the Jamestown Settlement Museum and the Yorktown Victory Center. Both include outdoor living history experience and indoor museums.

Educational programs offered at Jamestown include: Living with the Indians, Life at Jamestown Settlement, Cultures in Contact, and Voyage to Virginia at the Jamestown Museum; and at Yorktown: Colonial Life, The Life of a Private, and Colonial Medicine. Information on rates and scheduling are available at the education office (804) 253-4939. Self-guided tours can be scheduled through the group sales office at (804) 253-4838.

In addition, the education office offers two free teachers' kits:

1. Jamestown Teachers' Kit—brief history of first permanent English settlement in the New World, life in a Powhatan village, some illustrations, bibliography, and suggested activities for students K–12.
2. Yorktown Teachers' Kit—brief account of events leading to and during the American Revolution, brief descriptions of

the life of a private, colonial life, and slave life, a map of
Revolutionary events in Virginia, a bibliography, and
suggested activities for students K–12.

Washington

**DEPARTMENT OF TRADE AND
ECONOMIC DEVELOPMENT**
Tourism Development Division
P.O. Box 42500
Olympia, WA 98504-2500
(800) 544-1800 (except HI)

**SEATTLE–KING COUNTY CONVENTION
AND VISITORS BUREAU**
520 Pike Street, Suite 1300
Seattle, WA 98101
(206) 461-5840

West Virginia

WEST VIRGINIA DIVISION OF TOURISM AND PARKS
1900 Kanawha Boulevard
Building 6, Room B564
Charleston, WV 25303-0317
(800) CALL-WVA (except AK, HI)

Wisconsin

WISCONSIN TOURISM
P.O. Box 7970
Madison, WI 53707
(800) 432-TRIP (US) or (800) 372-2737 (IL, IA, MI, MN)

ICE AGE TRAIL FOUNDATION
101 W. Wisconsin
Pewaukee, WI 53072
(608) 691-2776

WISCONSIN DELLS VISITOR AND CONVENTION BUREAU
701 Superior Street
P.O. Box 390
Wisconsin Dells, WI 53965-0390
(608) 254-8088

■ Offers teachers a booklet, *Wisconsin Dells in Words and Pictures,* and a *1998 Wisconsin Dells Travel and Attraction Guide.* Wisconsin Dells Visitor and Convention Bureau also has a free educational video, called *Fun Facts,* that they loan to schools. Contact them to preview it.

GREATER MILWAUKEE CONVENTION AND VISITORS BUREAU
510 West Kilbourn
Milwaukee, WI 53203
(800) 231-0903

Wyoming

GRAND TETON NATIONAL PARK
P.O. Drawer 170
Moose, WY 83012
(800) CALL-WYO

WYOMING ROAD AND TRAVEL INFORMATION
Cheyenne, WY 82002
(307) 635-9966

CASPER AREA CHAMBER OF COMMERCE
500 North Center
Casper, WY 82601
(307) 234-5311

Chapter Five

Math

 Students often have strong feelings about math. Some of them seem to really like it—many of them seem to strongly dislike it. Math is arguably the most difficult subject to teach because students have so many misconceptions about it. This frustration (or feelings about its irrelevance) is ironic, because of all the subjects taught in school, math is arguably the one most connected to the "real world." After all, math is used at a cash station, a football game, and the grocery store (not to mention some of the more complex applications). Teachers have the burdensome responsibility of knowing they can introduce math in a way that either grips students or alienates them—often for a lifetime.

Thankfully, there are methods to teaching math "properly"— in a way that students will not only truly understand but will also enjoy. By using manipulatives, having students write explanations of how answers were obtained, and teaching the steps to problem-solving—shifting education from memorizing theorems to teaching skills and tools of analysis, observation, and critical thinking—students will understand math.

This process includes hands-on activities that one can do in the classroom to make abstract mathematical concepts tangible. The following resource section offers deals that will help with the process of teaching this potentially exciting subject.

Math Resources

CENSUS BUREAU EDUCATION PROGRAM

Attn: Dorothy Jackson
Data User Services Division
Washington, DC 20233-8300
(301) 763-1510

■ Offers a packet of free resources to help you teach statistics and U.S. population. The packet includes an activity book for students grades 5–12, *Statistics Aren't Static*, which can not only be used in math, but across the curriculum in history, economics, science, and geography. Other resources include two booklets on teaching students grades 1–12 about population trends.

Ask for: Free packet of free resources.
Requirements: None.

D.C. HEATH AND COMPANY

125 Spring Street
Lexington, MA 02173
(800) 235-3565

■ *Can You Find the MATH?* consists of a free poster and teacher guide featuring Kool D—Math Detective. Kool D—Math Detective uses clues about math in the real world—and finds examples everywhere (e.g., in forestry, pottery, fast food, designing, music, life-saving emergencies, courier delivery). Highly recommended.
Also from D.C. Heath:

• Heath Mathematics Connections: a comprehensive K–8 mathematics program

• Math Every Day: a hands-on, manipulative-based primary program

• Every Day Counts: day-by-day activities and resources for levels K–5

• Adventures in Thinking: critical-thinking activities for individual and small-group work for levels 3–8

- *Making the Case for Math*: a free practical report explaining the NCTM Curriculum and Evaluation Standards
- *Math for the 90s*: a free action guide for instructional leaders
- *Helping Your Child Learn Math with Activities for Children Aged 5 through 13*: a U.S. Department of Education and Office of Educational Research and Improvement book available from D.C. Heath by calling (800) 334-3284 (fax: (800) 824-7390). Copies of the book and pricing information are available at the same numbers. A package of five copies may be ordered using code number 37679-5. Shipping and handling charges will be added to your order.

Ask for: *Can You Find the MATH?* guide and poster and information about other programs listed above.

Requirements: None.

SCIENCE, MATHEMATICS, AND ENVIRONMENTAL EDUCATION (SE)
The Ohio State University
1929 Kenny Road
Columbus, OH 43210-1080
(614) 292-0263 or (800) 276-0462;
fax: (614) 292-0263; website: ericse@osu.edu

■ Don't forget to access ERIC (see Chapter 8) for math resources. You will be able to download many information resources, digests, studies, journals, and articles.

KAROL MEDIA
350 North Pennsylvania Avenue
P.O. Box 7600
Wilkes-Barre, PA 18773-7600
(717) 822-8899

■ *The Challenge of the Unknown*, a seven-part video, with a teaching guide, is available from Phillips Petroleum Company. It shows people using mathematics as a tool to make their tasks easier.

Ask for: *The Challenge of the Unknown* free video and teaching guide for math.

Requirements: Send letter on school stationery, indicating which title you want. Ask for a listing of additional titles.

NCTM
Dept M-I
1906 Association Drive
Herndon, VA 22091-1593
(703) 620-9840

■ Offers a free catalog of new math materials and classroom ideas dedicated to improving the teaching of mathematics.

Ask for: Free catalog.

Requirements: State which grade you teach.

Math Magazines and Periodicals

DYNAMATH
(800) 724-6527

■ Available from the school division of *Scholastic.* Filled with many different activities that involve all strands of math. Children in grade 5 particularly like this magazine. Nine issues are sent each school year.

GAMES JUNIOR
P.O. Box 10147
Des Moines, IA 50347

■ A challenging and fun magazine of all different kinds of games that give children hours of "brain workouts." Appropriate for ages seven and up.

"What Should I Expect from a Math Program?"

The National Council of Teachers of Mathematics (NCTM) has recently endorsed standards by which math should be taught in the elementary and middle-grade years. These standards have also been heavily endorsed by the business community. These endorsements, together with the technological advances of our society and the lack of math confidence in our workforce, have combined to produce tremendous support for the standards.

These standards make some assumptions about the way math should be taught and what parents might see when visiting the classroom. Here are some examples:

1. Children will be engaged in discovering mathematics, not just doing many problems in a book.

2. Children will have the opportunity to explore, investigate, estimate, question, predict, and test their ideas about math.

3. Children will explore and develop understanding for math concepts using materials they can touch and feel, either natural or manufactured.

4. The teacher will guide the students' learning, not dictate how it must be done.

5. Children will have many opportunities to look at math in terms of daily life and to see the connections among math topics such as between geometry and numbers.

6. Children will be actively involved in using technology (calculators and computers) to solve math problems.

The complete list of standards is available from NCTM, 1906 Association Drive, Reston, VA 22091-1593, (800) 235-7566.

GAMES MAGAZINE
P.O. Box 10147
Des Moines, IA 50347

■ The adult version of *Games Junior* (see above). Older children may prefer this magazine to *Games Junior*.

PUZZLEMANIA
Highlights
P.O. Box 18201
Columbus, OH 43218-0201
(614) 486-0631

■ A magazine that includes puzzles involving words, logical thinking, hidden pictures, spatial reasoning, etc.

ZILLIONS
Consumer Reports
P.O. Box 54861
Boulder, CO 80322

■ Children's version of *Consumer Reports* magazine. Shows math in the real world and offers children the opportunity to see how gathering data and information can lead to good decision making.

Chapter Six

Arts and Materials

"Especially in austere times, the arts must be nurtured, for it is our humanity that is at stake . . . art makes order out of chaos from a society which is, at the same time, foolish, intense, volatile, and potentially dangerous. It is art that is one generation's legacy to the next and attempt to define the present and to reveal the future."

—SUMMER INSTITUTE MEMBERS AT THE NATIONAL GALLERY OF ART

 Art materials and other supplies needn't be expensive. The deals listed in this section show where and how to obtain inexpensive materials. We have emphasized deals that are creative and environmentally safe.

Beyond the deals themselves, however, is an important concept: there are many ways to obtain free or very inexpensive materials, products, and supplies. Where? Often right in your own community. Talk to the owners of local stores or companies and ask for cardboard, paints, supplies, plants, furniture, etc. Talk to the community relations department in the companies and corporations near your school. These departments often have community resources built into their budgets—and need to connect with a school to make contributions!

Don't let these opportunities slip away. We have listed many, many resources throughout this chapter and this book, but make it a rule of thumb to continue to always look for the resources all around you.

Arts and Materials Supply Sources

BARGAIN HUNTING IN THE BAY AREA
Wingbow Press
7900 Edgewater Drive
Oakland, CA 94621
(510) 632-4700; fax: (510) 632-1281

■ One of the best ways to obtain free or low cost materials is to get involved in retail outlet buying. Sally Socolich's book, *Bargain Hunting in the Bay Area*, is famous in the California area. On our "things we'd like to see" list is a similar book for every area throughout the nation. If there isn't a similar book for your area, take these tips from Socolich: locate your warehouse district; follow the special closing sales; and shop out of season and save materials for later (e.g., shop for holidays after the holiday, enjoy the 50 percent off, and save the materials for next year).

Ask for: Ordering information.

Requirements: Cost of book.

CENTER FOR SAFETY IN THE ARTS
5 Beekman Street
New York, NY 10038
(212) 227-6220

■ Offers a 17″ × 22″ poster, "Safer Substitutes in Art," that lists more than 100 materials used in art projects and safety precautions and materials that can be substituted to make art projects safer.

Ask for: "Safer Substitutes in Art" poster.

Requirements: $5.00.

CHICAGO SCHOOL RECYCLE CENTER (CSRC)

Amy L. Peterson, Director

P.O. Box 148204

Chicago, IL 60614

(312) 348-1392

■ In this program, arts and materials meet recycling and business-education partnerships. CSRC organizes mutually beneficial efforts between industries, teachers, parents, and community that promote recycling and enrich educational programs. Business and industry donate their excess by-products, overruns, and rejects to schools, which in turn use the materials as educational resources. In this way, businesses solve their disposal problems while contributing to education (and use the donations as write-offs). Teachers are able to obtain *free* materials, and are thus encouraged to develop creative approaches to curriculum. Children receive hands-on experiences.

In addition to distributing free materials, CSRC offers teacher in-service training, parent workshops, and children discovery workshops.

Ask for: Further information.

Requirements: None.

CRAYOLA DREAM-MAKERS

P.O. Box 21187

Lehigh Valley, PA 18002-1187

(610) 253-6271

■ Crayola's art education program contains a 32-page art activities guide, posters, art activities tips, a techniques booklet, and other teacher resources. Program varies from year-to-year. Previous programs have included time-traveling, imagination, and visual worlds themes and are often still available.

Ask for: Crayola Dream-Makers kit.

Requirements: $2.00.

CREATE-A-CRAFT SCHOOL GRANT PROGRAM
1100-H Brandywine Boulevard
P.O. Box 2188
Zanesville, OH 43702-2188
(800) 294-5680

■ You can apply for the Association of Crafts and Creative Industries (ACCI) Create-a-Craft School Grant Program. If selected, you will receive videos, take-home activity sheets, project guides for various arts skills including airbrush, painting, and jewelry making. Materials are designed for beginning (K–6), intermediate (6–8), and advanced (8–12).

Ask for: Application.

Requirements: Application details requirements.

CREATIVE EDUCATIONAL SURPLUS
9801 James Circle, Suite C
Bloomington, MN 55431
(612) 884-6427 or (800) 886-6428

■ Creative Educational Surplus began when a group of educators were frustrated that they were unable to obtain suitable educational materials to match their needs and pocketbooks. The company features high quality materials salvaged from industry. (Your satisfaction is guaranteed; no matter how unique the materials are, they will be useful.) Many of the materials come with idea and activity cards.

Items include: Trays, latex gloves, *huge* grocery bags, "fun filters," three-yard-long nets, brushes, plastic pizza wheels, vinyl, transparent film (for inexpensive art aprons), masking tape, fifteen feet of numbers (for mathematical concepts), sandpaper, plugs of astroturf, large snaps on vinyl (eye-hand coordination), "glamorous" white gloves, plastic bowls, trays (various sizes), and canisters.

Creative Educational Surplus hopes you will share your ideas with them so other educators may benefit.

 **Recycling Notes and Tips**

Creative Educational Surplus shares its expertise:

> One of the best ways to recycle is to reuse materials instead of discarding them. Many typical "throwaways" can be used to enhance the learning/play environment of young children. In fact, "throwaways" often make better learning materials than do toys chosen from catalogs or stores. The best learning environments for young children are characterized by a large amount of open-ended, nonspecific materials—materials like boxes, large sheets of paper, and Styrofoam chips or other packing materials—things that are often thrown away. Such materials can be used in almost unlimited ways and are generally inexpensive, free, donated, or found.
>
> Materials that can be used in a variety of non-specific ways are often referred to as "open-ended materials." Such materials offer the following benefits . . . they: (1) foster creativity and frequently lead to more complex play, (2) are low cost and easy to get, (3) are interesting to children, (4) are frequently donated by parents (if asked), thus increasing family involvement in the program.

Following is a list of typical "throwaways" with open-ended characteristics:

- boxes, especially big appliance boxes
- large pieces of cloth (bedspreads, sheets, blankets)
- rope, yarn, string
- buckets, plastic jugs, foam food containers
- tool boxes, fishing tackle boxes, sorting trays, assorted luggage
- wood scraps, old magazines, wallpaper books, rug scraps

> In addition to using "throwaways," you may also wish to seek out suppliers who specialize in surplus materials.
>
> How can you and your peers add to this list? How many different materials and activities can you make from what raw materials?

Ask for: Quarterly publication.

Requirements: None.

DEPARTMENT OF TEACHER AND SCHOOL PROGRAMS
Education Division
National Gallery of Art
Washington, DC 20565
(202) 842-6880

■ A new directory of teacher programs in more than 250 art museums across the United States and Canada is now available from the National Gallery of Art. A free resource for teachers, school administrators, librarians, and museum professionals, *Teacher Programs in Art Museums: A Directory* is the first text publication issued by the National Gallery in computer diskette format only.

The directory contains information about teacher workshops and in-service programs as well as summer programs lasting a few days to a month. Programs in art education and interdisciplinary studies are included, and institutions offering university or in-school credit are identified. The directory is available on diskette for the Macintosh computer. It requires Hypercard 2.1 or later and System 6.0, with two to three megabytes of RAM, or System 7 with four to five megabytes of RAM. The National Gallery's survey of teacher programs in art museums and the publication were made possible by the Bauman Foundation and the Circle of the National Gallery of Art.

Ask for: Free computer diskette of *Teacher Programs in Art Museums: A Directory.*

Requirements: Send request on school or institution letterhead.

HOHNER, INC.
Lakeridge Park
101 Sycamore Drive
Ashland, VA 23005-9998
(804) 550-2700; fax: (804) 550-9625

■ What arts program is complete without music? Write for information on how to obtain Hohner's RB106 harmonica instruction course specifically designed for elementary school children. This program has been tested in several public school systems and has been a tremendous success. Includes song book and Rainbow harmonica.

Ask for: RB106 harmonica instruction course.

Requirements: None.

ALASKA CRAFT
17000 Tideview Drive
Anchorage, AK 99516-4833
(907) 345-1621

■ Alaska Craft is a remarkable operation that offers easy craft kits and small gifts of high value for a low price, which can be used by school children, teachers, Scout leaders, and families. The kits can be used across the curriculum in arts, math, science, social studies, geography, writing, and history. They contain reusable patterns; you can buy one and combine patterns with your own materials or buy several materials-included kits . . . still for a dollar each! A flyer that lists their craft kits and sample are available by writing to the above address. Examples include:

• Preprinted snowflake patterns, ready to fold and cut, can be used as a hands-on science activity.

A Writing-Arts Activity for Justa Dollar Materials

Sharon Hamlen of Alaska Craft/Justa Dollar shares an activity that teachers have successfully used.

1. Order a flyer and sample from Justa Dollar to become familiar with products.
2. Pick three items from the flyer that the students can use for an art project.
3. List the items and the Justa Dollar address on the board, and have the students choose an item. The students bring in their own dollar.
4. Next, have the students write Justa Dollar and request the item, explaining why it appeals to them and what they plan to do with the project after they have made it or what they hope to learn by doing this project.
5. When the packages arrive, the excitement begins. The package will bring a built-in art activity.
6. Complete the art activity.

- A tangram puzzle provides hours of quiet diversion or can be used with a tangram unit to teach math.
- Eskimo children patterns (running, hunting, ice fishing, with sled dog) can be used in social studies, history, or geography units.
- Generous volcanic ash sample in a clear glass bottle can be a great prize (a terrific conversation piece and collector's item) or be part of a science activity (students feel and then examine the sample under a microscope).
- A Pin Punch note kit makes an elegant prize, arts project, or history lesson about the pioneers, who often used pin punch to decorate. For your dollar, you will obtain three sheets of

paper with matching envelopes, nine full-sized patterns, punch pin, and full directions.

- A Pin Punch angel pattern rings in an old-fashioned lesson on how the pioneers decorated, celebrated Christmas, and made art images.

Ask for: Flyer and sample.

Requirements: $1.00.

KIDSART
P.O. Box 274
Mt. Shasta, CA 96067
Telephone and fax: (916) 926-5076

■ Publishes inexpensive art enrichment units. They currently have 25 units on a variety of art topics. These 16-page, reproducible booklets sell for $3.00 (when ordered one-by-one) or less (in sets and by subscription). KidsArt also sells art books, materials, and resources for elementary art teaching—unusual, hard-to-find, and especially good items. All items are recommended.

Also offers a free resource . . . the KidsArt Mail Art Exchange program. Kids, as individuals or in class groups, send decorated "art envelopes" and letters to KidsArt, which pairs them with other students across the country, and sends each child's entry to the other. The kids then have each other's address, and go on to exchange further pen pal letters on their own. The only cost for this program is the two first-class postage stamps they require with each entry and which are used to return each pen pal letter and envelope. Some of the art is incredible, and seven years of the Mail Art Exchange is archived on 35mm slides at KidsArt.

Ask for: Information on enrichment units and the Art Exchange program.

Requirements: None.

PRO CHEMICAL & DYE, INC.

P.O. Box 14

Somerset, MA 02726

(508) 676-3838 or (800) 2 BUY DYE (orders only)

■ In an effort to increase safety in art production, Pro Chemical & Dye, Inc. offers a free catalog to introduce teachers to non-toxic permanent dyes and inks for marbling, tie-dye, printing, dyeing, and painting.

Ask for: Free catalog, and inquire about dye workshops.

Requirements: None.

THE UNIVERSITY PRINTS

21 East Street

P.O. Box 485

Winchester, MA 01890

(617) 729-8006; fax: (617) 729-8024

■ Visual materials for Art History studies. Scholarly and inexpensive, these materials are useful for historical or comparative study and for large or small class enrollment. Immediate shipment. Available materials include:

- 7,500 Basic Art History Subjects in 5.5" prints. Sent individually or in sets.
- Visual Textbooks of an instructor's selection of subject for any course are collated without charge. Cost is based on the per-print price (7¢ each in black and white, 15¢ each in color, or in special sets).
- *Free University Prints Complete Catalogue*, Visual Textbook samples for any course, or Visual Survey for library reference.

Ask for: Free *University Prints Complete Catalogue* and order form.

Requirements: None.

A Good Deal . . . and a Good Idea

Art Supplies for Kids (ASK) grants provide assistance to K–12 teachers who buy art supplies for their classes with their own funds. The grants are in the form of gift certificates redeemable at any of the four Amsterdam Art stores located in the San Francisco Bay Area. They have granted approximately $10,000 since March 1993. The funds designated for grants come from customer donations that Amsterdam Art matches dollar-for-dollar with the help of art supply manufacturers. Amsterdam Art also holds fundraising events (such as children's art shows and sales, and at-counter ASK candy sales). Amsterdam Art wants to help teachers stop spending their own money on these supplies . . . and asks why other art supply stores around the country don't follow their lead. . . . For further information, write or call: ASK Administrator, Amsterdam Art, Discount Art Supplies, 1013 University Avenue, Berkeley, CA 94710, (510) 649-4800.

VISUAL MANNA
Box 553
Salem, MO 65560
(314) 729-2100

■ Offers an art curriculum that supports core subjects through hands-on art, visually teaching subjects such as grammar basics and writing. Publishes a project newsletter featuring seasonal projects for children.

Ask for: Free sample lesson and brochure.

Requirements: None.

Lions Has a Deal for You

The Lions Club sponsors a Peace Poster Contest for students ages 11–13. The theme varies. An example from a previous year is "Journey to Peace," wherein the winner received a cash award of $1,500 and took a tour of the United Nations in New York City with two family members. Students must be sponsored by their local Lions chapter. To find your local Lions chapter and for more information call (800) 288-8846.

THE WOOLIE WORKS
Dept. BH
6201 E. Huffman Road
Anchorage, AK 99516
(907) 345-0553

■ Offers for free a package of brightly colored "postals," which can be used as note cards or postcards. Class sets can be requested. A sister company to Justa Dollar, The Woolie Works offers similar art kits for just $1.00. This is another company that has established a network of product supply and uses almost all recycled products. Art kits include:

• Victorian Box Kit: a fun craft to keep your students busy on a rainy day. With just a little folding and cutting, you can make a pretty Victorian box for holding small items. Kit includes brightly colored and patterned paper (enough to make three boxes) plus instructions and ribbon.

• Christmas Candle: an easy cut-and-glue kit. Candle is made from a clothespin, bright red ribbon, a gold "flame," red berries, and green holly. Use this idea to make many more candles. Illustrated instructions.

- Mini Finger Mouse: contains materials to make a mini finger mouse puppet, just right for vacation car trips. Mouse-making materials and illustrated instructions are included.
- Paper Sculpture Butterfly: three-dimensional butterfly. An easy cut-and-fold project. Make several for a mobile or attach to a magnet. The pattern can be reused to make additional butterflies from magazine papers free of writing or from colorful gift wrap. Reduce or enlarge pattern for different sizes.
- Picture Frames: kit includes four die-cut mini-frames 4″ × 5″, the perfect size for school pictures. Frames are cut from brightly colored or printed papers, ready to use as they are, stencil, or hand paint.
- Butterfly Mobile: make this bright plastic mobile from the three plastic butterflies, string, and stick that are included in the kit. Illustrated directions.

Ask for: Specific item (listed above), or illustrated price list.

Requirements: None.

Chapter Seven

Science, Health, and Environment

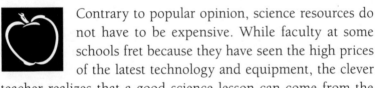

Contrary to popular opinion, science resources do not have to be expensive. While faculty at some schools fret because they have seen the high prices of the latest technology and equipment, the clever teacher realizes that a good science lesson can come from the things all around us. Children love to explore—to make hypotheses about the world around them and then prove or disprove them. The science lesson is an excellent place for students to explore their senses and the world, becoming expert observers while developing their critical thinking.

Science can be fun and meaningful, as it offers tremendous hands-on opportunities to learn valuable lessons about the effects of humankind on the environment. A science lesson can also incorporate lessons from other major subject areas.

Luckily, many people and organizations are eager to provide creative opportunities to explore the processes that make up this subject area. Herein are terrific opportunities to work with great companies and groups who not only have a vested interest in the world around them, but also offer tremendous educational kits to help teachers instruct kids about the great world of science.

Under the vast science umbrella, which includes the study

of the earth, the universe, and the human body, we have included resources on health and the environment. These free and inexpensive resources will help students learn more about how to protect themselves and the world they are inheriting.

Science and Environmental Resources

AMERICAN COAL FOUNDATION (ACF)
1130 17th Street, NW, Suite 220
Washington, DC 20036
(202) 466-8630

■ The American Coal Foundation has an amazingly rich packet of science-energy-environment information, including: "What Everyone Should Know About Coal Gasification," "What Everyone Should Know About Coal," "Electricity from Coal," "Land Reclamation," "Coal: Ancient Gift Serving Modern Man," "Power from Coal Activity Book," "Let's Learn About Coal" (two-sided poster), "Power from Coal" (teacher's guide), and "Coal Science Fair Ideas." They also have a film loan (sample titles: *Acid Rain: No Simple Solution* and *Balancing Needs: Coal and the Environment*). ACF also produces and distributes "Understanding the Greenhouse Effect" slide presentation (discounted to $25.00 for teachers), which includes 53 numbered slides, script, teacher's guide, summary, and brochure.

Ask for: Teacher's packet.

Requirements: Requests must be on school stationery.

AMERICAN RADIO RELAY LEAGUE (ARRL)
Education Activities Department
225 Main Street
Newington, CT 06111
(860) 594-0200

■ The ARRL provides a list of local radio enthusiasts who can help you listen to the astronauts on missions! Select students will get the opportunity to talk with astronauts who are in space. Package also includes free lesson plans and activity sheets for use when following shuttle missions.

Ask for: Astronaut listings and packet.

Requirements: None.

COUSTEAU SOCIETY
870 Greenbrier Circle, Suite 402
Chesapeake, VA 23320-2641
(800) 431-4395

■ Offers a free copy of the Cousteau Society's *Dolphin Log*, a bimonthly science and environmental magazine written for students 7–13 years old.

Ask for: Free sample of *Dolphin Log*.

Requirements: Postage and handling, $1.00. $10.00 for subscription, $28.00 for family membership.

DON'T LET A GOOD THING GO TO WASTE
(800) 438-5856

■ A free recycling program from the Plastic Bag Association. Gets kids thinking about trash and ways to cut down on waste.

Ask for: Don't Let a Good Thing Go to Waste.

Requirements: Materials targeted for grades 2–5.

EARTH FORCE'S WILDLIFE PROTECTION CAMPAIGN
1501 Wilson Boulevard, 12th Floor
Arlington, VA 22209
(703) 243-7400

■ Offers free action guide for kids, which encourages youth groups and teachers to become involved in wildlife protection campaigns.

Ask for: Free action guide.

Requirements: None.

ELEMENTARY EQUIPMENT GIFT PROGRAM
U.S. Department of Energy
Office of Science Education Programs
1000 Independent Avenue S.W.
Washington, D.C. 20585
(202) 208-1797

■ Thanks to the Department of Energy, K–12 educators can obtain used excess equipment such as computers, computer peripherals, and general science lab equipment. For more information you can contact Dr. Larry Barker on e-mail at Larry.Barker@ hq.doe.dov or phone him at (202) 586-4947.

Ask for: Information on the Elementary Equipment Gift Program and an application.

Requirements: Application.

FLEXIBLE PACKAGING ASSOCIATION
1090 Vermont Avenue, NW, Suite 500
Washington, DC 20005-4960
(202) 842-3880

■ Offers a creative package of lessons—absolutely free—titled *Less Waste in the First Place*, which details the history of packaging and demonstrates how to reduce waste. As a final activity, students design creative waste-reducing packages. Also includes a list of organizations students can write to on their own to obtain further information about packaging and recycling.

Ask for: Less Waste in the First Place.
Requirements: Targeted grades 5–9.

HANDS-ON SCIENCE MATERIALS
National Academy Press
2101 Constitution Avenue, NW, Box 285
Washington, DC 20055
(800) 624-6242

■ Obtain this 176-page teaching guide of hands-on science materials for elementary schools from both the United States and abroad. Listings include human biology, health, life science, earth science, physical science, and applied science.

Ask for: *Science for Children: Resources for Teachers.*

Requirements: $9.95 (plus $4.00 postage and handling). A discount is available for multiple copies.

HUMANE SOCIETY'S *STUDENT ACTION GUIDES*
P.O. Box 362
East Haddam, CT 06423-0362

■ Guides help students learn how they can protect the earth and its animals, and offer tips for creating an environmental protection club with many activities to get others involved.

Ask for: *Student Action Guides.*

Requirements: Targeted for grades 7 and up.

KEEP AMERICA BEAUTIFUL, INC.
Mill River Plaza
9 West Broad Street
Stamford, CT 06902
(203) 323-8987

■ A resource for seeds (for schools, communities, and those in need), information on how to beautify the country (recycling, waste management), and a program called *Preserving Our National Heritage.*

Ask for: Packet for teachers.

Requirements: None.

KIDS FACE ILLUSTRATED
P.O. Box 158254
Nashville, TN 37215

■ Club membership in Kids FACE club is free. Join Kids for a Clean Environment, receive the information-packed newspaper, and *get involved.*

Ask for: *Kids FACE Illustrated* and club membership.

Requirements: Indicate how many copies you'd like to receive.

KODAK'S USING CAMERAS IN THE CURRICULUM
(800) 242-2424

■ Kodak sponsors this program wherein students learn about the environment and their community via photography. If your class is selected to participate, you will receive a 35-mm class camera, 35 single-use cameras, teaching guide, a poster, questionnaires, and other valuable materials. Call for more information.

Ask for: "Using Cameras in the Curriculum" information.

Requirements: None.

MAGNIFICENT MUM EDUCATION PROGRAM
Customer Service
Yoder Brothers, Inc.
P.O. Box 230
Barberton, OH 44203
(800) 321-9573

■ This program on mums features a teacher resource kit and 50 plant cuttings. Projects include hands-on experiments, growing program, and beautification.

Ask for: Magnificent Mum.

Requirements: For grades K–1, 2–3, or 4–5. $9.95 plus $1.50 for handling.

MR. WIZARD'S FREE SCIENCE TV
(800) 258-2344

■ *Teacher to Teacher with Mr. Wizard,* an educational science television series we recommend, is free via *Cable in the Classroom* on Nickelodeon. (For more information on *Cable in the Classroom,* see Chapter 8.) Broadcasts show outstanding teachers effectively teaching science. Students will see their peers excited by the learning process. Call for information, a free monthly newsletter, and more.

NATIONAL AERONAUTICS AND SPACE ADMINISTRATION (NASA)
Elsie Weigel
NASA Education Division
Educational Publications Branch
Code FEP
300 E Street, SW, Room 2-J34
Washington, DC 20546
(202) 358-0000

■ Offers free triannual newsletter titled *Educational Horizons,* which lists NASA mission updates, planned shuttle launches, NASA workshops, and more free resources for teachers.

Ask for: Membership for *Educational Horizons.*

Requirements: Mention that you are a teacher.

NASA'S SPACE VIDEO
NASA CORE
15181 Route 58 South
Oberlin, OH 44074
(216) 774-1051, ext. 293

■ Offers an inexpensive video for early elementary students that demonstrates daily life aboard the space shuttle. Also includes a resource guide of classroom activities.

Ask for: *"Living in Space."*

Requirements: $10.00 plus $3.50 postage and handling.

NATIONAL COALITION FOR AVIATION EDUCATION
P.O. Box 28086
Dept. I
Washington, DC 20038

■ Teaching aviation? Obtain this free booklet, *A Guide to Aviation Education Resources.*

Ask for: Free booklet.

Requirements: None.

NATIONAL ENERGY INFORMATION CENTER

Energy Information Administration
Room 1F-048
Forrestal Building
100 Independence Avenue, SW
Washington, DC 20585
(202) 586-8800

■ Get the free booklet *Energy Education Resources: Kindergarten Through 12th Grade,* which lists more than 75 sources for free or inexpensive energy education materials, including teacher's guides, catalogs, posters, and booklets.

Ask for: *Energy Education Resources* booklet.

Requirements: None.

NATIONAL GARDENING ASSOCIATION

Youth Garden Grants
180 Flynn Avenue
Burlington, VT 05401
(802) 863-1308

■ Win a grant for your school! Awards grants of plants, seeds, tools, and gardening supplies with an estimated value of $500.

Ask for: Application.

Requirements: Send your name and school's name, address, and phone number to the above address. Your school must have a gardening program involving 15 or more students (ages 3–18).

NATIONAL SCIENCE TEACHERS ASSOCIATION (NSTA)

Publications
1742 Connecticut Avenue, NW
Washington, DC 20009
(202) 328-5800

■ Offers two free booklets on careers in science teaching (one for students and one for adults). Also offers free NSTA position statements, information on NSTA activities, and applications for various programs for competition.

Ask for: Ask for specific item from above.

Requirements: None.

NUTRI-ART
Makers of Nutritional Games
6210 Ridge Manor Drive
Memphis, TN 38115

■ Designs and sells nutrition education materials at a reasonable cost. Materials cover a thematic area that could fit a number of various objectives in science (or art), including lessons in color matching, visual discrimination, reading, health, and the body. Products include Fat Cookie Card Game, Food Shuffle, Nutritionally for You, and a coloring book.

Ask for: Free catalog.

Requirements: None.

PHILLIPS PETROLEUM COMPANY
Educational Films
Karol Media
P.O. Box 7600
Wilkes-Barre, PA 18773-7600

■ Obtain a free video *A Home for Pearl* to help teach elementary students about pollution and wildlife. A teacher's guide (with activities) is included.

Ask for: *A Home for Pearl.*

Requirements: For elementary-grade teachers.

RECYCLING RESOURCES
United States Conference of Mayors
1620 Eye Street, NW
Washington, DC 20006

■ Learn how to develop a school recycling program by recycling materials students use daily, such as milk cartons and newspapers. Request free packet and receive a book of tips on establishing a recycling program, guidelines for receiving a certificate of achievement, an activities booklet, and a recycling-in-schools newsletter.

Ask for: Recycling kit.

Requirements: None.

TANIGUCHI FOUNDATION
99 East Basse, Suite 180
San Antonio, TX 78209
(210) 822-8547

■ Funds a gardening and art guide called *Let's Grow Pizza*, promoting environmental education for classrooms. Children have a "being there" experience with the life cycle, and learn of growth in plants as a parallel to the growth in other forms of nature.

Ask for: A free packet of information on Sprout Scouts.

Requirements: None.

TEACHERS INSURANCE AND ANNUITY ASSOCIATION (TIAA)
485 Lexington Avenue, 27th Floor
New York, NY 10017
(888) 842-8001

■ Offers a free color poster of apples grown in the United States. The back of the poster has information on TIAA financial service and life insurance.

Ask for: Apple Poster.

Requirements: None.

TROPICAL TRIBUNE
J.C. McKenna Middle School
307 South 1st Street
Evansville, WI 53536

■ Subscribe to the *Tropical Tribune* and have your students learn about preserving the rain forests.

Ask for: Subscription to the *Tropical Tribune*.

Requirements: Targeted for students grades 3 and up. $1.00 per subscription.

U.S. COUNCIL FOR ENERGY AWARENESS
Suite 400
1776 Eye Street, NW
Washington, DC 20006-3708
(202) 293-0770

■ Offers pro-nuclear information kits that show one side of this controversial subject, which should help kids (and adults) make a more informed choice about nuclear energy.

Ask for: Nuclear Energy: Good News for the Environment and Energy Independence information kit.

Requirements: None.

USDA FOREST SERVICE
P.O. Box 96090
Washington, DC 20090-6090
(800) 699-6637

■ Offers various information packets for incorporating forestry into the school curriculum.

Ask for: Agriculture Information Bulletin No. 426, *Understanding the Game of the Environment,* "Why Leaves Change Color" and "What Do We Get from Trees" posters.

Requirements: None.

A WORLD IN MOTION PROGRAM
SAE Foundation
400 Commonwealth Drive
Warrendale, PA 15096-0001
(800) 457-2946, weekdays, 4:00–7:00 P.M. (EST)

■ Want to make 4th, 5th, and 6th grade science, math, and physics fun? If you can find a scientist or engineer (e.g., a friend, parent, or interested community member) who'll help you conduct the program via class visits, the SAE Foundation will enroll you in its free A World in Motion program. (The first thing to do is read the registration brochure titled *Let's Get Acquainted*.) Following registration, you'll receive a kit that includes a teacher's guide, posters, a video, cooperative learning projects, and experiments students can do independently.

Ask for: A World in Motion program.

Requirements: A partner. For grades 4–6.

General Energy Information Resources

AMERICAN PETROLEUM INSTITUTE

Public Affairs Department
1220 L Street, NW
Washington, DC 20005
(202) 682-8000

EDISON ELECTRIC INSTITUTE

701 Pennsylvania Avenue, NW
Washington, DC 20005
(202) 508-5000

ENVIRONMENTAL PROTECTION AGENCY

Public Information Center
401 M Street, SW
Washington, DC 20460
(800) 490-9198

GLOBAL CLIMATE COALITION

1275 K Street, NW
Washington, DC 20004
(202) 682-9161

NASA PUBLIC AFFAIRS
Washington, DC 20546
(202) 358-1764

NATIONAL COAL ASSOCIATION
Public Affairs Department
1130 17th Street NW, 8th Floor
Washington, DC 20546
(202) 463-2625

U.S. DEPARTMENT OF ENERGY
1000 Independence Avenue, SW
Washington, DC 20585
(800) 874-2884

Alternative Energy and Recycling Resources

ADOPT-A-STREAM FOUNDATION
P.O. Box 5558
Everett, WA 98206
(206) 388-3487

■ Dedicated to teaching stream revival.

Ask for: Basic information, blue sheet, and fish button.

Requirements: $1.00 and a self-addressed, stamped envelope (SASE).

AMERICAN CHEMICAL SOCIETY
1155 16th Street, NW, Suite 814
Washington, DC 20036
(800) 227-5558; fax: (202) 872-8068

Ask for: Free copy of *WonderScience* magazine.

Requirements: Send or fax your name and address to above address.

AMERICAN INSTITUTE OF BAKING
1213 Bakers Way
Manhattan, KS 66502
(913) 537-4750 or (800) 633-5137; fax: (913) 537-1493

Ask for: *Bread in the Making* booklet (written at an approximate 4th grade reading level).

Requirements: 50¢ per copy plus postage.

AMERICAN SOLAR ENERGY SOCIETY
2400 Central Avenue, Suite G-1
Boulder, CO 80301
(303) 443-3130; fax: (303) 443-3212

■ Dedicated to advancing the use of solar energy.

Ask for: Sample copy of *Solar Today*.

Requirements: None.

AMERICAN WIND ENERGY ASSOCIATION
777 North Capitol Street, NE, Suite 805
Washington, DC 20002
(202) 408-8988

■ Dedicated to promoting wind as an economical and technically viable energy source.

Ask for: Wind energy fact sheets.

Requirements: None.

ASTRONOMICAL SOCIETY OF THE PACIFIC
Teachers' Newsletter, Dept. N.
390 Ashton Avenue
San Francisco, CA 94112
(415) 337-1100; hotline: (415) 337-1244

■ A free newsletter on teaching astronomy in primary and secondary schools offered by the four leading professional astronomy societies in North America. Designed to help teachers,

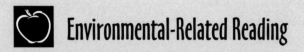

Environmental-Related Reading

COME BACK, SALMON
How a Group of Dedicated Kids Adopted Pigeon Creek and Brought It Back To Life, by Molly Cone with photographs by Sidnee Wheelwright; a Sierra Club Book.

curriculum specialists, and librarians include more astronomy in their classroom work, this newsletter is produced by the non-profit Astronomical Society of the Pacific and is co-sponsored by the American Astronomical Society, the Canadian Astronomical Society, and the International Planetarium Society. Each issue features:

- clear nontechnical articles on new developments in the exploration of the universe
- practical classroom activities for teaching astronomy
- specific suggestions for the best written and audiovisual resources on astronomical topics

The newsletter focuses on a variety of interesting subjects in astronomy, such as the exploration of the planets, exploding stars, the search for life elsewhere, the Big Bang, and the difference between astronomy and astrology. No background in astronomy is assumed of the reader; in fact, the sponsoring societies particularly want to encourage teachers who have not had much training in science to write for the newsletter.

Ask for: To be put on the mailing list for future issues.

Requirements: Teachers or school librarians should write on school stationery and identify the grade level they teach.

BUTTERBROOKE FARM
78 Barry Road
Oxford, CT 06483

■ An organic farm dedicated to "food and seeds for people, not for profit." Gardening guides, a gardening video, and seed co-op membership also available. Great resource for beginning a school or community gardening project.

Ask for: Sample garden seed collection.

Requirements: $1.00 for postage and handling.

CLOUD CHART, INC.
P.O. Box 21298
Charleston, SC 29413-1298
(803) 577-5268

Ask for: Information on cloud charts for weather unit studies.

Requirements: None.

CONSERVATION AND RENEWABLE ENERGY INQUIRY AND REFERRAL SERVICE (CAREIRS)
P.O. Box 3028
Merrifield, VA 22116
(800) 523-2929

■ Provides information to the public on the full spectrum of renewable energy technologies and energy conservation.

Ask for: Fact sheets, brochures, bibliographies, information on solar, ocean, and wind energy, and a condensed list of CAREIRS publications.

Requirements: Limit your requests from the condensed list to eight titles per order. You may make copies, as the information is within the public domain.

ENERGY AND MARINE CENTER

P.O. Box 190
9130 Old Post Road
New Port Richey, FL 34673
(813) 848-4870

■ Instructions on how to build a solar-powered hot dog cooker. This hot dog cooker has been field-tested extensively and works well.

Ask for: Solar hot dog cooker directions.

Requirements: Send your request, a business-size SASE, and 25 cents.

GREENPEACE PUBLIC INFORMATION

1436 U Street, NW
Washington, DC 20009
(202) 319-2444, weekdays, 9:30 A.M.–5:30 P.M. (EST)

■ Greenpeace will send you a free catalog on how to raise overall environmental awareness, how to obtain publications and videos, and how to use their store to:

Reduce
- dependence on fossil fuel
- use of nonrecyclable products
- unnecessary packaging
- use of dangerous chemicals

Reuse
- grocery bags
- glass bottles and jars
- containers and wrapping

Recycle
- newspapers
- glass

- aluminum
- computers
- cardboard

Ask for: Free catalog.

Requirements: None.

JOLLY TIME

The American Pop Corn Company
Box 178
Sioux City, IA 51102
(712) 239-1232; fax: (712) 239-1268

■ Sample teacher's information kit on popcorn is available free of charge upon request. Also offers a history book on the American Pop Corn Company and Jolly Time Pop Corn products and a full-color recipe booklet. Perhaps best of all is the popcorn activity guide which uses popcorn as a hands-on material to teach science, history, math, geography, home economics, and health.

Ask for: Teacher's Packet.

Requirements: None.

NASA CORE

NASA CORE/Lorain County JVS
15181 Routes 58 & 20
Oberlin, OH 44074
(800) 621-0660

■ NASA has established a Central Operation of Resources for Educators (CORE) that functions as a national clearinghouse for aerospace information and materials relating to many curriculum areas. In addition to catalogs for teachers, they have added a children's catalog and included space-related items, which they will mail to youngsters.

Ask for: Catalog of available information, materials, and items.

Requirements: State whether you are a student or teacher.

NATIONAL ARBOR DAY FOUNDATION
100 Arbor Avenue
Nebraska City, NE 68410
(888) 448-7337

■ A nonprofit education organization dedicated to tree planting and environmental stewardship. Publishes a variety of unique education materials that are available for free or are offered at reproduction and shipping costs. Learn about Arbor Day and its history from publications that provide information, ideas, and activities for planning a ceremony.

Ask for: Teacher's packet for Arbor Day celebration.

Requirements: None.

NATIONAL COALITION AGAINST
THE MISUSE OF PESTICIDES
701 E Street, SE, Suite 200
Washington, DC 20003
(202) 543-5450

■ Offers information packet on cleaning up pesticides in schools, including *Cry Out: An Illustrated Guide to What You Can Do to Save the Earth*, a publication about energy, water, toxins, and pollutants.

Ask for: Environmental information.

Requirements: None.

THE NEW EXPLORERS
c/o NASA-CORE/Lorain County JVS
15181 Route 58 South
Oberlin, OH 44074
(800) 621-0660

■ *The New Explorers* is a public television series that has taken millions of viewers to the modern frontiers of science. All episodes from the series are available for purchase on VHS. Each videotape is accompanied by a comprehensive teacher's guide filled with high-interest activities.

Ask for: New Explorers ordering information.

Requirements: Cost per videotape (including teacher's guide) is $34.95 plus shipping and handling. Teacher's guide is also available separately (for $14.95) for those educators taping the series off the air.

PARTNERSHIP FOR PLASTICS PROGRESS
1275 K Street, NW, Suite 500
Washington, DC 20005
(800) 2-HELP-90 or (202) 223-0125

■ Offers educational materials on plastics, including *How to Set Up a School Recycling Program* and a 12-minute videotape *The Resource Revolution*, with a teacher's guide, which explores the present and future of plastics recycling. Activity sheets and one video and booklet per school.

Ask for: Information on available print and video materials.

Requirements: None.

POLYSTYRENE PACKAGING COUNCIL
1025 Connecticut Avenue, NW, Suite 515
Washington, DC 20036
(202) 822-6424

■ Dedicated to polystyrene recycling programs. Looks at the role plastics have in everyday lives.

Ask for: The Plastic and the Environmental Sourcebook. Classroom activities.

Requirements: None.

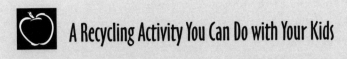

A Recycling Activity You Can Do with Your Kids

RECYCLE FOOD SCRAPS

Recycle food scraps from lunch by creating an outdoor compost pile or an indoor worm bin. You provide the worms food and a place to live, they will produce rich organic soil from food waste. Worms and starter information can be obtained from these sources.

GARDENER'S SUPPLY
128 Intervale Road
Burlington, VT 05401
(800) 444-6417

WORMS WAY
3151 South Highway 446
Bloomington, IN 47401
(800) 274-9676

THE WORM CONNECTION
580 Erbes Road
Thousand Oaks, CA 91362
(805) 496-2872

STEEL CAN RECYCLING INSTITUTE
680 Andersen Drive
Pittsburgh, PA 15220
(800) 876-SCRI

■ Free materials for teachers, including learning sheets and material on steel cans and multimaterial recycling efforts.

Ask for: Information for teachers.

Requirements: Specify grade level(s) you teach.

TREES FOR LIFE, INC.
1103 Jefferson
Wichita, KS 67203
(316) 945-6929; fax: (316) 263-5293

■ Creates educational activities based on the conviction that in this age of adequate resources and technology, there is no reason for people to suffer hunger and starvation. Trees for Life fights malnutrition and hunger and can help our neighbors become self-sufficient.

They provide management and education to people in developing countries for the planting and care of fruit and fuel trees. Current projects are in India, Nepal, Brazil, and Guatemala, where more than 14 million fruit and fuel trees have been planted since 1984. In addition to planting trees, some other projects include providing fuel-efficient stoves to reduce the use of woods and improve the quality of life for villagers. They also place beehives in some villages alongside tree-planting work to enhance the fruit production of the trees and to provide honey for families.

Trees for Life has developed an educational program for U.S. students—a tree-growing kit that can be used as a class or individual project. (The class project is the Tree Adventure Kit, the individual's project is a Tree Kit.) It teaches children about the importance of trees through hands-on experience. More than two million children have participated in this project.

Ask for: Free coloring sheet and information on the Tree Adventure Kit.

Requirements: Send a business-size SASE with a request.

USA RICE COUNCIL
P.O. Box 740121
Houston, TX 77274
(713) 270-6699; fax: (713) 270-9021

■ A nonprofit, non-branded association that represents the U.S. rice industry. Funding comes from rice farmers in the U.S. rice-growing states of Arkansas, California, Louisiana, Mississippi,

A "Pre-cycling" Activity You Can Do with Your Kids

A GARBAGE EXPERIMENT
BY EKNATH EASWARAN*

I was amazed to read that every man, woman, and child in our country generates twice his or her weight in waste every day. This garbage habit affects not only our own country. Our growing refuse pile now spills over our borders through what is called "garbage imperialism." As our landfills fill up, we are sending our waste, much of it toxic, to poor third world countries desperate for the meager income it brings.

So I suggest that all of us perform a little experiment. Keep a waste journal. It's a very good project for children, and an even better project for adults, to observe and calculate how this mountain of waste is generated. Then gradually cut down your waste from two times your weight to one. Generate only enough waste to equal your weight. If you are more ambitious, you can reduce your weight. This has nothing to do with capitalism or socialism or any other -ism; this has everything to do with love of children. Every child everywhere is entitled to the reasonable comforts of life. No child's country should be treated as a dump.

How many ways can you "pre-cycle": . . . stop waste by not creating any?

* (Reprinted by permission)

Missouri, and Texas. Promotes the consumption of U.S.-grown rice throughout the United States and the world.

Offers a variety of brochures for the classroom, most of which are recipe and nutrition oriented. A general rice informational brochure, "Facts About U.S. Rice," gives an overview of the U.S. rice industry and includes information on history, production, nutrition, cooking, and more. Other titles include "The Many Nationalities of Rice," "Sport Sense, The Common Sense Approach to a Healthful Lifestyle," and "Teaching the Fun Way . . . with Rice! (activities using rice)."

Ask for: To obtain single or classroom quantities of the brochure, send a request asking for the particular brochure(s) and specify how many are needed.

Requirements: None.

Health and Safety Resources

AMERICAN ASSOCIATION OF ORTHODONTISTS
401 North Lindbergh Boulevard
St. Louis, MO 63141-7816
(314) 993-1700; fax: (314) 997-1745

■ Provides free booklets to teachers. Helps students learn about orthodontic health.

Ask for: Free information for teachers.
Requirements: None.

AMERICAN OPTOMETRIC ASSOCIATION
Communications Center
243 North Lindbergh Boulevard
St. Louis, MO 63141
(314) 991-4100; fax: (314) 991-4101

■ Offers five pamphlets to help students learn about their changing bodies and good health.

- "A Teacher's Guide to Vision Problems"
- "Your Preschool Child's Eyes"
- "Your School-Age Child's Eyes"
- "A Look at Reading and Vision"
- "Toys, Games, and Your Child's Vision"

Ask for: Teachers may request single copies of each pamphlet.

Requirements: The pamphlets are free. Send a business-size SASE.

DOLE FOOD CO., INC.
155 Bovet Road, Suite 476
San Mateo, CA 94402
(800) 232-8888

■ Provides free CD-ROM program titled "5 Day Adventures," which encourages kids to "eat smart."

Ask for: "5 Day Adventures" CD-ROM.

Requirements: Request on school letterhead. State whether your CD-ROM drive is a Macintosh system or MS-DOS/Windows. State the number of CD-ROM disks you need.

EARTHQUAKE AWARENESS KIT
Movers & Shakers (A-4)
State Farm Insurance Company
1 State Farm Plaza
Bloomington, IL 61710-0001
(309) 766-2311

■ This K–12 earthquake preparedness kit contains a safety video (in entertaining sitcom-style), a classroom poster, and lesson plans that teach group cooperation, safety, critical thinking, and decision making.

Ask for: Free Earthquake Awareness Kit.

Requirements: Send your name, school name, and address on school letterhead.

FREE SPIRIT PUBLISHING, INC.

400 First Avenue North, Suite 616
Minneapolis, MN 55401
(800) 735-7323; website: help4kids@freespirit.com

■ With its inception in 1983 by Judy Galbraith, Free Spirit Publishing became the first publishing house to focus exclusively on helping kids cope with the challenges they face in school, at home, and with peers. A former teacher of gifted children and teens, Galbraith believed that the publishing world could play a key role in helping kids help themselves.

Here are four books you will find genuinely interesting:

• *Succeeding with LD*
• *Teaching Your Gifted Children in the Regular Classroom*
• *When Can I Get a Tattoo? And 95 Other Questions (and Answers) About Teen Rights and the Law*
• *What Do You Stand for: A Kid's Guide to Building Character*

Ask for: Free catalog.

Requirements: None.

GAS APPLIANCE MANUFACTURERS ASSOCIATION

(800) GAMA-811

■ Offers a free resource kit containing an activity guide, stickers, and a comic book that teaches about the safe use and storage of flammable liquids.

Ask for: Free teacher's kit.

Requirements: For teachers of students grades 4 and above.

HEALTHY GROWING UP

McDonald's USA/Ronald McDonald Children's Charities
(800) 627-7646

■ A life skills program for grades K–3 that focuses on growing up healthy. Reproducible lessons on exercise, self-esteem, nutrition, and overall health. Endorsed by the Society for Nutrition and the President's Council on Physical Fitness and Sports.

Ask for: Growing Up Healthy.

Requirements: $10.00.

METLIFE
Health and Safety Education
1 Madison Avenue
New York, NY 10010-3690
(212) 578-2211

■ Offers many free and low-cost resources to help students and their families. Many of the resources feature MetLife's trademark "Peanuts" comic strip characters. (Resources available in both English and Spanish.) Other resources include "Health and Safety Educational Materials," which consists of a health pamphlet, nutrition guide cookbook, statistical bulletins, cards, and various informational material.

Ask for: Free resources and price list for healthy living pamphlets and other information.

Requirements: None.

POWER BITES—DENTAL INFORMATION VIA DINOSAURS!
American Association of Orthodontists
401 North Lindbergh Boulevard
St. Louis, MO 63141-7816
(314) 993-1700; fax: (314) 997-1745

■ The American Association of Orthodontists and Scholastic Inc. have teamed up to bring you this teaching program. Provides teachers, students, and parents with current, straightforward information on dental care and orthodontics. Packed with fascinating dinosaur lore to spark student interest in teeth. For instance, some dinosaurs had teeth that just wouldn't quit—when the old ones wore down, new ones came in to take their place.

The program includes:

• background material on teeth—dinosaur and human

- teaching suggestions to introduce students to the important role teeth play in human life
- activities that include learning about the function of teeth and the importance of braces
- a resource list of easy-to-find information on teeth and dental health
- reproducible take-home materials for parents

Ask for: Power Bites.

Requirements: None.

Chapter Eight

ERIC and the New Technology

 Technology has become part of all of our lives. These days, even the most "high-tech" technology is often user-friendly and accessible. And what better way to bring learning into the 21st century than to integrate technology and curriculum?

The new technology shouldn't frighten anyone—software is simply a new medium on which curriculum is published. You may already have classroom access to television, videocassettes, CDs, laserdiscs, or software, and if so, you know these are readily accessible to you with a minimal amount of effort and familiarity.

Other resources can also help make technology work for you and keep you up to date in your profession. The Educational Resources Information Center (ERIC) is one of the most important of these. This federally funded, nationwide information network is designed to provide you with, among other things, ready access to education literature.

As the following pages show, worlds of opportunity and great deals exist for educators who want to use new technology to do an even better job.

Accessing the Leading Edge: Introducing ERIC

What Is ERIC?

At the heart of ERIC is the largest education database in the world—containing more than 800,000 records of journal articles, research reports, curriculum and teaching guides, conference papers, and books. Each year approximately 30,000 new records are added. The ERIC database is available in many formats at hundreds of locations.

ERIC presents education information in a convenient format. More than 20 years ago, ERIC became the first commercial online database. In 1986 the ERIC database became available for searching on CD-ROM (compact disk, read-only memory).

Now ERIC is at the forefront of efforts to make education information available through computer networks, and it is available to thousands of teachers, administrators, parents, students, and others through electronic networks, including the Internet, CompuServe, America Online, America Tomorrow, and GTE Educational Network Services. Network users can read and download information on the latest education trends and issues. On some systems, users can direct education-related questions to AskERIC and get a response from an education specialist within 48 hours.

ERIC also offers customized assistance through a network of subject-specific education clearinghouses that provide toll-free reference and referral, and free or low-cost publications on important education topics.

The ERIC system, managed by the U.S. Department of Education's Office of Educational Research and Improvement (OERI), consists of 16 clearinghouses, a number of adjunct clearinghouses, and additional support components.

The ERIC Clearinghouses collect, abstract, and index education materials for the ERIC database, respond to requests for information in their subject areas, and produce special publications on current research, programs, and practices.

The ERIC Document Reproduction Service (EDRS) produces

and sells microfiche and paper copies of documents announced in the ERIC database.

The ERIC Processing and Reference Facility is the technical hub of the ERIC system and produces and maintains the database and systemwide support products.

ACCESS ERIC coordinates ERIC's outreach, dissemination, and marketing activities, develops system-wide ERIC publications, and provides general reference and referral services.

The following information will help you understand how you can use the resources available from ERIC to meet your needs.

What Does ERIC Offer You?

- Toll-free numbers that put you in touch with subject-specific clearinghouses.
- More than 1,000 two-page research synthesis publications—available in print and electronic formats.
- A 48-hour turnaround, electronic question-answering service.
- Access from your personal computer.
- Hundreds of lesson plans you can access and download to your computer.
- Document ordering via fax or toll-free phone call.

Where Can You Use ERIC?

You can access ERIC in a number of places.

1. Personal computers
2. The Internet
3. Libraries and Information Centers
4. ERIC Clearinghouses

Let's look at the above four resources in deeper detail.

PERSONAL COMPUTERS

If you have a personal computer with a modem, you can use it to access ERIC information. Commercial online services such as America Online, CompuServe, and GTE Educational Network

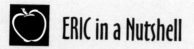 **ERIC in a Nutshell**

ERIC is a method of opening the gates to a giant network of educational information:

ACCESS ERIC
2277 Research Boulevard
Rockville, MD 20850
(800) LET-ERIC (538-3742);
E-mail: acceric@inet.ed.gov;
website: http://www.aspensys.com/eric

Services all feature AskERIC information on current topics in education. Many of these services offer all or part of the ERIC database, which can be searched using key words, titles, authors, or other approaches.

A personal computer and modem can also be used to search ERIC and many other databases for a fee by signing up with commercial online database vendors such as Bibliographic Retrieval Services (BRS) or DIALOG Information Services.

Online Vendors

BRS INFORMATION TECHNOLOGIES
8000 Westpark Drive
McLean, VA 22102-9980
(800) 955-0906 or (703) 442-0900; fax: (703) 893-4632

DATA-STAR/DIALOG
Plaza Suite
114 Jermyn Street
London SW1Y 6HJ
England
011-44 71 930 7646; fax: 011-44 71 930 2581

DIALOG INFORMATION SERVICES
3460 Hillview Avenue
Palo Alto, CA 94304
(800) 334-2564 or (415) 858-2700; fax: (415) 858-7069

GTE EDUCATIONAL NETWORK SERVICES
5525 MacArthur Boulevard, Suite 320
Irving, TX 75038
(800) 927-3000 or (214) 518-8500; fax: (214) 751-0964

ONLINE COMPUTER LIBRARY CENTER (OCLC)
6565 Frantz Road
Dublin, OH 43017-0702
(800) 848-5878 or (614) 764-6000; fax: (614) 764-6096

CD-ROM Vendors

DATA-STAR/DIALOG
Plaza Suite
114 Jermyn Street
London SW1Y 6HJ
England
+44 71 930 7646; fax: +44 71 930 2581

EBSCO PUBLISHERS
83 Pine Street
P.O. Box 2230
Peabody, MA 01960-7250
(800) 653-2726 or (508) 535-8500; fax: (508) 535-8523

NATIONAL INFORMATION SERVICES CORPORATION (NISC)
Wyman Towers, Suite 6
3100 St. Paul Street
Baltimore, MD 21218
(410) 243-0797; fax: (410) 243-0982

ORYX PRESS
4041 North Central Avenue
Suite 700
Phoenix, AZ 85012-3397
(800) 279-ORYX or (602) 265-2651; fax: (800) 279-4663
or (602) 265-6250

SILVERPLATTER INFORMATION, INC.
100 River Ridge Drive
Norwood, MA 02062-5026
(800) 343-0064 or (617) 769-2599; fax: (617) 769-8763

THE INTERNET

The Internet is a worldwide cooperative computer network made up of many smaller networks that are interconnected. You may access the Internet through a university, statewide teacher or community computer network, or your membership with a commercial service. Internet users can reach AskERIC for fast, individualized responses to education questions and a free electronic education library. For questions about education, child development and care, parenting, learning, teaching, information technology, and other related topics, send an E-mail message to: askeric@ericir.syr.edu.

You can also use the Internet to connect to sites that offer free public access to the ERIC database. For the latest information on Internet access to ERIC, contact the ERIC Clearinghouse on Information and Technology at (800) 464-9107; E-mail: askeric@ericir.syr.edu; or ACCESS ERIC at (800) LET-ERIC; E-mail: acceric@inet.ed.gov.

LIBRARIES AND INFORMATION CENTERS

ERIC is available at most university libraries, many public libraries, and other professional libraries and education resource centers—more than 1,000 of which are designated as ERIC information service providers. At these locations, you can search the ERIC database yourself or ask a librarian to search for you. Most of these locations also have a substantial ERIC microfiche collection and microfiche readers/printers for making copies of ERIC documents.

ERIC CLEARINGHOUSES

All of the ERIC Clearinghouses have toll-free numbers and information specialists to help you. Even if you have access to ERIC on your personal computer or at a convenient library, you may want to contact the clearinghouse that covers the education topic you're researching. Clearinghouses offer free and inexpensive publications and tips on how to search the ERIC database and often refer you to other sources of information. (See complete listing of ERIC Clearinghouses later in this chapter.)

Who Uses ERIC?

ERIC is the largest education resource in the world and serves the information needs of a wide spectrum of users, including:

Teachers—to obtain the latest information on pre-service and in-service training, learn about new classroom techniques and materials, and discover resources for personal and professional development.

Administrators/School Boards—to identify new and significant education developments, learn new management tools and practices, and assist local and state agencies in planning education programs.

Students—to gain access to the latest information for preparing term papers, theses, and dissertations, obtain information on career development, and build a personalized, low-cost education library.

Parents/General Public—to learn about new developments in education, gain information on the role of parents and the public in child development and school improvement, learn about adult continuing education, and keep abreast of new legislation on education.

Researcher/Professors—to keep up to date on research and practice, avoid duplication of research efforts, and obtain full text research reports.

Librarians/Information Specialists—to compile bibliographies and summaries on specific education topics, search the ERIC database for answers to queries, and locate and order documents.

Professional Organizations—to keep members abreast of trends and issues in specific areas of education and obtain current information for association publications and position statements on education issues.

Journalists—to gather background information, provide resources for articles and programming, and monitor trends and issues in education.

What Can You Get from ERIC?

Whether you need a little information or a lot, ERIC is an excellent resource for research summaries on current, high-interest topics, reference to recent journal articles, complete research reports, books, or curriculum guides, or extensive bibliographies.

REFERENCE AND REFERRAL SERVICES

ERIC offers free reference and referral services to the public through its network of clearinghouses, ACCESS ERIC, and electronic AskERIC question-answering services. Staff are available to provide ERIC publications, answers questions about ERIC, locate hard-to-find documents, and refer you to other appropriate information sources. Call an ERIC Clearinghouse if you have a subject-specific question. As mentioned earlier, call ACCESS ERIC for help in using the ERIC system or for the latest information on electronic AskERIC services.

Publications Produced by ERIC

The ERIC system produces more than 250 special publications each year. These publications provide you with the latest research and practice information on current, high-interest topics.

Clearinghouses produce free and low-cost publications including brochures, newsletters, pamphlets, monograph series, and bibliographies. ERIC Digests, which are two-page research syntheses, are among the ERIC system's most popular offerings.

There are currently more than 1,000 Digests, and approximately 100 new titles are produced each year. For information on clearinghouse publications, see the list of ERIC Clearinghouses later in this chapter.

The ERIC Database

The ERIC database has bibliographic information and abstracts on two types of materials: ERIC documents (with ED numbers) and journal articles (with EJ numbers). To see if ERIC is for you, the easiest way to begin is to call, write, fax, or access ERIC at:

ACCESS ERIC
1600 Research Boulevard
Rickville, MD 20850-3172
(800) LET-ERIC (538-3742) or (301) 251-5264;
fax: (301) 251-5767; E-mail: acceric@inet.ed.gov

■ Ask for *All About Eric*, the information source from which this chapter was formed. Or, you can use the information provided herein to access the clearinghouses and adjunct clearinghouses to access ERIC directly.

Looking into the Future

With the expansion of computer access to information, interest in full-text, electronic access to ERIC documents and articles, which allows users to print or download the complete text of files, has increased. The ERIC system is exploring ways to make more of the database available in full text and has already made the popular ERIC Digests available through the ERIC Digests Online File. You can get complete copies of ERIC Digests from many electronic sources, including most CD-ROM versions of ERIC, online vendors, and several Internet hosts.

Until electronic full text becomes available for other ERIC database references, you can find most ERIC Documents at any library that has the ERIC microfiche collection. At these locations you can read the publications and make copies for a nominal per-page charge on a microfiche reader/printer. To locate the microfiche collection nearest you, call ACCESS ERIC at (800) LET-ERIC.

You can also purchase microfiche or paper copies of most ERIC documents from the ERIC Document Reproduction Service (EDRS), which accepts orders by phone, fax, mail, or online (through DIALOG, BRS, OCLC). For more information or to order documents, contact EDRS.

ERIC DOCUMENT REPRODUCTION SERVICE (EDRS)

7420 Fullerton Road, Suite 110
Springfield, VA 22153-2852
(800) 443-ERIC or (703) 440-1400; fax: (703) 440-1408

■ Copies of journal articles announced in ERIC can be found in library periodical collections, through interlibrary loan, or from article reprint services, such as those listed here.

INSTITUTE FOR SCIENTIFIC INFORMATION (ISI)

Genuine Article Service
3501 Market Street
Philadelphia, PA 19104
(800) 523-1850 or (215) 386-0100; fax: (215) 386-6362

■ To obtain journals that do not permit reprints and are not available at your library, write directly to the publisher. Publishers' addresses are listed in the front of each issue of *Current Index to Journals in Education* (CIJE), ERIC's printed index of journal citations, which is available in many libraries.

UNIVERSITY MICROFILMS INTERNATIONAL (UMI)

Article Clearinghouse
300 North Zeeb Road
P.O. Box 1346
Ann Arbor, MI 48106-1346
(800) 521-0600, ext. 2786 or (313) 761-4700;
fax: (313) 665-7075

Some Questions to Ask Before Jumping onto ERIC

1. What is the best way to access the ERIC database?

2. How much will it cost? You may have free or inexpensive access to ERIC. If not, you may have to pay for connect time on some computer systems or order a search through a search service.

3. How much of the ERIC database is available? Some services provide access to the entire ERIC database, which goes back to 1966; others may allow you to search only the last five or ten years of ERIC. If this is important to you, find out how much of ERIC is available before choosing a search system.

4. How long will it take? Turnaround time can vary from a few minutes, if you have direct access to ERIC on a personal computer, to several days or longer if you have to order a search that someone else conducts.

5. How much flexibility does the search system offer? Many different software systems are used to search ERIC. Some menu-driven search systems make it easy for a first-time user, but may limit opportunities to make changes to the search question.

Using the Thesaurus of ERIC Descriptors

Before you run an ERIC search, it is important to take a few minutes to find the ERIC descriptors that best capture your topic. For example, articles and documents about the development of children's social skills would be indexed under the descriptor *interpersonal competence*. The ERIC descriptor for children at risk is *at-risk persons*. When you search for information about high school students, you can use the descriptor *high school students*, but you would miss a lot of material if you did not also use the descriptor *secondary education*.

Locations that offer ERIC searches should have reference copies of the *Thesaurus of ERIC Descriptors*, and some search systems allow access to the *Thesaurus* while running your search. If you cannot locate a copy of the *Thesaurus*, call the ERIC Clearinghouse that covers your subject and ask for help with search strategy.

The *Thesaurus* is essential for any site that offers access to ERIC. It is the master list of ERIC's nearly 10,000 subject headings used in indexing and searching. To get the best results from an ERIC search, users should start by converting their search questions to the most appropriate ERIC descriptors. The *Thesaurus* includes complete cross-reference structures and rotated and hierarchical displays. To order the *Thesaurus*, call Oryx Press at (800) 279-ORYX.

Contributing to the ERIC Database

If you have recently authored a research report, program description or evaluation, literature review, teaching guide, conference paper, or other education-related work, you can make it permanently available and accessible to others through ERIC.

If you are uncertain which clearinghouse is appropriate or if you have questions about submitting your work, contact:

ERIC PROCESSING AND REFERENCE FACILITY
Acquisitions Department
1301 Piccard Drive, Suite 300
Rockville, MD 20850-4305
(800) 799-ERIC or (301) 258-5500; fax: (301) 948-3695;
E-mail: ericfac@inet.ed.gov

ERIC Clearinghouses

Each of the 16 ERIC Clearinghouses specializes in a different subject area of education. The clearinghouses acquire significant literature within their particular scope, select the highest quality and most relevant materials, and catalog, index, and abstract them for input into the database. The clearinghouses also provide research summaries, bibliographies, information analysis papers, and many other products and services. Together, the clearinghouses present the most comprehensive mosaic of education information in the country.

ADULT, CAREER, AND VOCATIONAL EDUCATION (CE)
Ohio State University
1900 Kenny Road
Columbus, OH 43210-1090
(800) 848-4815 or (614) 292-4353; fax: (614) 292-1260;
E-mail: ericacve@magnus.acs.ohio-state-edu

ASSESSMENT AND EVALUATION (TM)
The Catholic University of America
210 O'Boyle Hall
Washington, DC 20064
(202) 319-5120; fax: (202) 319-6692;
E-mail: eric_ae@cua.edu

COMMUNITY COLLEGES (JC)
3051 Moore Hall
University of California at Los Angeles
Los Angeles, CA 90024-1521
(800) 832-8256 or (310) 825-3931; fax: (313) 206-8095;
E-mail: eeh3usc@mvs.oac.ucla.edu

COUNSELING AND STUDENT SERVICES (CG)
University of North Carolina at Greensboro School of
Education
1000 Spring Garden Street
Greensboro, NC 27412-5001
(800) 414-9769 or (919) 334-4114; fax: (919) 334-4116;
E-mail: ericcass@iris.uncg.edu

DISABILITIES AND GIFTED EDUCATION (EC)
Council for Exceptional Children
1920 Association Drive
Reston, VA 22091-1589
(800) 328-0272 or (703) 264-9474; fax: (703) 264-9494;
E-mail: ericec@inet.ed.gov

EDUCATIONAL MANAGEMENT (EA)

University of Oregon
1787 Agate Street
Eugene, OR 97403-5207
(800) 438-8841 or (503) 346-5043; fax: (503) 346-2334;
E-mail: ppiele@oregon.uoregon.edu

ELEMENTARY AND EARLY CHILDHOOD EDUCATION (PS)

University of Illinois
805 West Pennsylvania Avenue
Urbana, IL 61801-4897
(800) 583-4134 or (217) 333-1386; fax: (217) 333-3767;
E-mail: ericeece@ux1.cso.uiuc.edu

HIGHER EDUCATION (HE)

George Washington University
One Dupont Circle NW, Suite 630
Washington, DC 20036-1183
(800) 773-3742 or (202) 296-2597; fax: (202) 296-8379;
E-mail: eriche@inet.ed.gov

INFORMATION AND TECHNOLOGY (IR)

Syracuse University
4-194 Center for Science and Technology
Syracuse, NY 13244-4100
(800) 464-9107 or (315) 443-3640; fax: (315) 443-5448;
E-mail: eric@ericir.syr.edu

LANGUAGES AND LINGUISTICS (FL)

Center for Applied Linguistics
1118 22nd Street, NW
Washington, DC 20037
(800) 276-9834 or (202) 429-9292; fax: (202) 659-5641;
E-mail: eric@cal.org

READING, ENGLISH, AND COMMUNICATION (CS)
Indiana University
Smith Research Center, Suite 150
2805 East 10th Street
Bloomington, IN 47408-2698
(800) 759-4723 or (812) 855-5847; fax: (812) 855-4220;
E-mail: ericcs@ucs.indiana.edu

RURAL EDUCATION AND SMALL SCHOOLS (RC)
Appalachia Educational Laboratory
1031 Quarrier Street
P.O. Box 1348
Charleston, WV 25325-1348
(800) 624-9120 or (304) 347-0400; fax: (304) 347-0487;
E-mail: u56e1@wvnvm.wvnet.edu

SCIENCE, MATHEMATICS, AND
ENVIRONMENTAL EDUCATION (SE)
Ohio State University
1929 Kenny Road
Columbus, OH 43210-1080
(614) 292-0263; fax: (614) 292-0263; E-mail: ericse@osu.edu

SOCIAL STUDIES/SOCIAL SCIENCE EDUCATION (SO)
Indiana University
Social Studies Development Center
2805 East 10th Street, Suite 120
Bloomington, IN 47408-2698
(800) 266-3815 or (812) 855-3838; fax: (812) 855-0455;
E-mail: ericso@ucs.indiana.edu

TEACHING AND TEACHER EDUCATION (SP)
American Association of Colleges for Teacher Education
One Dupont Circle NW, Suite 610
Washington, DC 20036-1186
(800) 822-9229 or (202) 293-2450; fax: (202) 457-8095;
E-mail: ericsp@inet.ed.gov

URBAN EDUCATION (UD)
Teachers College, Columbia University
Institute for Urban and Minority Education
Main Hall, Room 303, Box 40
525 West 120th Street
New York, NY 10027-9998
(800) 601-4868 or (212) 678-3433; fax: (212) 678-4048;
E-mail: eric-cue@columbia.edu

ADJUNCT CLEARINGHOUSES

Adjunct ERIC Clearinghouses are associated with the ERIC Clear-inghouse that overlaps the narrower scope of the adjunct. Each adjunct identifies and acquires significant literature within its scope area. The clearinghouse with which the adjunct is associated then catalogs, indexes, and abstracts the documents for inclusion in the ERIC database. Like the larger clearinghouses, the adjuncts provide free reference and referral services in their subject areas.

ADJUNCT ERIC CLEARINGHOUSE FOR
ART EDUCATION
Indiana University
Social Studies Development Center
2805 East 10th Street, Suite 120
Bloomington, IN 47408-2698
(800) 266-3815 or (812) 855-3838; fax: (812) 855-0455;
E-mail: ericso@ucs.indiana.edu

ADJUNCT ERIC CLEARINGHOUSE ON CHAPTER 1 (COMPENSATORY EDUCATION)

Chapter 1 Technical Assistance Center
PRC, Inc.
2601 Fortune Circle East
One Park Fletcher Building, Suite 300-A
Indianapolis, IN 46241-2237
(800) 456-2380 or (317) 244-8160; fax: (317) 244-7386

ADJUNCT ERIC CLEARINGHOUSE ON CLINICAL SCHOOLS

ERIC Clearing on Teaching and Teacher Education
American Association of Colleges for Teacher Education
One Dupont Circle NW, Suite 610
Washington, DC 20036-1186
(800) 822-9229 or (202) 293-2450; fax: (202) 457-8095;
E-mail: iabdalha@inet.ed.gov

ADJUNCT ERIC CLEARINGHOUSE FOR CONSUMER EDUCATION

National Institute for Consumer Education
207 Rackham Building, West Circle Drive
Eastern Michigan University
Ypsilanti, MI 48197-2237
(800) 336-6423 or (313) 487-2292; fax: (313) 487-7153;
E-mail: cse_bonner@emunix.emich.edu or
edu_bannister@emuvax.emich.edu

ADJUNCT ERIC CLEARINGHOUSE FOR ESL LITERACY EDUCATION (LE)

Center for Applied Linguistics
1118 22nd Street, NW
Washington, DC 20037
(202) 429-9292, ext. 200; fax: (202) 659-5641;
E-mail: ncle@cal.org

ADJUNCT ERIC CLEARINGHOUSE FOR
LAW-RELATED EDUCATION (LRE)
Indiana University
Social Studies Development Center
2805 East 10th Street, Suite 120
Bloomington, IN 47408-2698
(800) 266-3815 or (812) 855-3838; fax: (812) 855-0455;
E-mail: ericso@ucs.indiana.edu

ADJUNCT TEST COLLECTION CLEARINGHOUSE
Educational Testing Service
Rosedale Road
Princeton, NJ 08541
(609) 734-5737; fax: (609) 683-7186;
E-mail: mhalpern@rosedale.org

NATIONAL CLEARINGHOUSE FOR
U.S.-JAPAN STUDIES (JS)
Indiana University
Social Studies Development Center
2805 East 10th Street, Suite 120
Bloomington, IN 47408-2698
(800) 266-3815; (812) 855-3838; fax: (812) 855-0455;
E-mail: ericso@ucs.indiana.edu

Federal Sponsor

EDUCATIONAL RESOURCES
INFORMATION CENTER (ERIC)
U.S. Department of Education
Office of Educational Research and Improvement (OERI)
555 New Jersey Avenue, NW
Washington, DC 20208-5720
(202) 219-2289; fax: (202) 219-1817;
E-mail: eric@inet.ed.gov

■ The ERIC Program staff manages the ERIC system, coordinates systemwide activities, and establishes policy.

Publishers

ORYX PRESS
4041 North Central Avenue, Suite 700
Phoenix, AZ 85012-3397
(800) 279-ORYX or (602) 265-2651;
fax: (800) 279-4663 or (602) 265-6250;
E-mail: arhjb@asuvm.inre.asu.edu

■ Oryx Press publishes *Current Index to Journals in Education* *(CIJE)*, the *Thesaurus of ERIC Descriptors*, and other ERIC products.

UNITED STATES GOVERNMENT PRINTING OFFICE (GPO)
Superintendent of Documents
P.O. Box 371954
Pittsburgh, PA 15250-7954
(202) 783-3238; fax: (202) 512-2250

■ GPO publishes *Resources in Education*.

How to Start an ERIC Collection

Libraries and resource centers can make ERIC available on a modest budget. The ERIC database is available in print, online, and on CD-ROM. Full-text copies of ERIC documents can be ordered either on microfiche or paper.

CD-ROM

Since 1986, when the ERIC database became available on CD-ROM, it has been extremely popular. CD-ROM technology allows vast quantities of data to be stored on compact disks, which are searchable at self-contained personal computer stations. To access the ERIC database on CD-ROM, you need a personal computer, a CD-ROM drive, and a subscription to one of the CD-ROM vendors (listed earlier in this chapter).

ERIC CD-ROM products are updated quarterly and sold on a set-fee, subscription basis, which makes them a cost-effective option for libraries that offer open access. Advances in networking technology allow multiple users to access a single CD-ROM database simultaneously; ask any vendor about a multiuse license.

ONLINE ACCESS THROUGH COMMERCIAL SERVICES

Online access to ERIC is available through several commercial vendors. Most of these vendors offer sophisticated search capabilities, the ability to access the entire ERIC database (from 1966 to the latest month) at once, and access to a host of other databases that may interest users. One must be trained in the vendor's search language to make use of the most powerful search capabilities, therefore this type of searching usually is performed by librarians or other professionals. Costs include membership fee, charges based on the number of minutes connected to the service, and the number of citations downloaded.

LOCALLY MOUNTED SYSTEMS

An increasing number of institutions, especially universities and state university systems, are mounting ERIC data on their mainframes for use by their clientele. The host institution bears the cost of maintaining the database, selects the search software, and determines its own access policies. In some cases, the ERIC database is linked to the library's online public access catalog (OPAC) and searched with the same interface. To buy the ERIC database tapes for programming and mounting, call the ERIC Processing and Reference Facility noted earlier in this chapter at (800) 799-ERIC.

ERIC TRAINING MATERIALS

ERIC Video

ERIC: In Action offers viewers a broad perspective on ERIC as their premier source for education information. The 15-minute video covers four major topics:

- basic structure
- major benefits

- key index features, and
- options for locating materials

ERIC: In Action is available for $15 from the ERIC Clearinghouse on Information and Technology.

ERIC Overhead Transparency Masters

ACCESS ERIC now offers a set of 33 ERIC overhead transparency masters that present an introduction to the database, describe the work of the ERIC Clearinghouses, and discuss electronic access to ERIC information. They are invaluable to librarians, professors, in-service directors, and others in need of ERIC training tools. The transparency masters (paper copies) are available free from ACCESS ERIC.

Training Materials from ERIC Clearinghouses

Many of the ERIC Clearinghouses produce training materials designed for specific audiences. For example, the ERIC Clearinghouse on Rural Education and Small School offers *A Parent's Guide to the ERIC Database*, and the ERIC Clearinghouse on Disabilities and Gifted Education produces *How to Use ERIC to Search Your Special Education Topic*. If you are interested in subject-specific materials that explain ERIC, contact the appropriate clearinghouses.

On-site Training

ERIC staff are available to conduct training programs, seminars, and workshops. If you have a group that could benefit from expert training on how to use ERIC, contact one of the clearinghouses or ACCESS ERIC.

Reference and Referral Directories

Catalog of ERIC Clearinghouse Publications

This catalog lists more than 1,400 current education titles, including teaching guides, bibliographies, research summaries, and monographs, published by the ERIC Clearinghouses. Many of the publications are free, others are available at a minimal cost. The *Catalog* also includes ordering information and prices and is available for $10.00 from ACCESS ERIC.

Directory of ERIC Information Service Providers

Research organizations, libraries, and schools will want a copy of this free directory for use by patrons and staff. It lists more than 1,050 agencies and organizations (including addresses, telephone numbers, and services available) that provide computerized searches of the ERIC database.

ERIC Directory of Education-Related Information Centers

The *Directory* identifies and describes 450 resource centers and other agencies that provide information synthesis, user services, technical assistance, information dissemination, or reference and referral services in education-related areas. The *Directory* is available in print, for $20.00, or on disk, $25.00, from ACCESS ERIC.

ERIC Calendar of Education-Related Conferences

The *Calendar* provides a chronological listing of the more than 525 international, national, and regional education-related conferences held each calendar year.

ERIC Indexes and Search Aids

A number of free and low-cost publications available from the ERIC Processing and Reference Facility are useful references for libraries and information centers that provide access to ERIC.

For pricing information and a complete list of available indexes and search aids, contact the ERIC Processing and Reference Facility.

The ERIC Review

This free journal provides education practitioners with research and news. Call ACCESS ERIC for more information.

A Pocket Guide to ERIC

This free, handy reference guide briefly describes the ERIC system. Bulk quantities are available from ACCESS ERIC for classroom, seminar, or conference use.

Other New Technology Resources

A+ AMERICA
(800) 557-2466

■ Offers a program wherein proof-of-purchase from various sponsors allows schools to obtain free software, computers, televisions, video cameras, and more. This year-round program is made up of different vendors for different states ranging from AT&T, MCI, Skippy, Apple, and Sony. Once you register your school, you will be provided with a Shopping Guide wherein you pick a target product for which to save. An excellent way to bring students and the entire community together for a clearly focused goal.

Ask for: Enrollment or information on A+ America.

Requirements: Must be part of a school.

CABLE IN THE CLASSROOM
1900 North Beauregard Street, Suite 108
Alexandria, VA 22311
(800) 743-5355

■ A public service arm of the cable television industry, Cable in the Classroom describes itself as

> Member cable companies providing free installation and basic service to all public- and state-approved private schools passed by cable. Some cable companies also offer satellite dishes at cost for those schools outside the delivery area; others offer complimentary subscriptions to *Cable in the Classroom* magazine. Further, they work with schools to encourage effective use of television through workshops and correspondence highlighting updated programming information.
>
> A part of that highway is Cable in the Classroom. Cable in the Classroom members are working to help teachers provide their students with both an expanded view of the world and with the skills they'll need to succeed in the 21st century.

Upon obtaining Cable in the Classroom, you will be able to access 27 cable channels (including HBO, PBS, MTV, C-Span, The Discovery Channel, and CNN). Support material is available upon request in both the traditional print medium or via a variety of fax and online services.

Ask for: Information on obtaining Cable in the Classroom.

Requirements: None.

CAMPBELL'S LABELS FOR EDUCATION PROGRAM
Campbell's Soup Company
Campbell Place
Camden, NJ 08103
(800) 257-8443

■ A program for schools and public libraries, in which participants collect Campbell's product labels to win big prizes. Schools are registered, and then receive a catalog from which teachers can choose prizes ranging from playground equipment to computers. For a million labels, a school can win a new van. That may seem like a lot, but schools can network with others (e.g., churches, community) to collect labels. It is a public relations task for the schools involved, but innovation could be the key to winning money and prizes for your school. While the actual program runs November through March, smart collectors collect year-round.

Ask for: Information on Campbell's Labels for Education Program.

Requirements: None.

CHILDREN'S SOFTWARE REVUE
520 North Adams Street
Ypsilanti, MI 48197-2482
(313) 480-0040

■ A bimonthly newsletter published by Active Learning Associates and targeted to teachers (and parents) of children age three to ten. The *Children's Software Revue* can be a tremendous help in

In the Digital Age, Your Classroom TV becomes a Gateway to the Information Superhighway.

The Learning Channel (TLC) offers "TLC Elementary School," with curriculum-based programming, and "Teacher TV," which showcases educators' solutions to various contemporary educational challenges. Call (800) 321-1832 for a free teacher's guide.

C-Span offers support material as well as scheduling information by calling a toll-free educators' hotline (800) 523-7586.

The Weather Channel offers an illustrated companion textbook/workbook to its *Weather Classroom* meteorology programs. The books are free; call for the price of shipping and handling. Teachers can also borrow videos (thirteen available at this publication) for 30 days, for shipping and handling expenses only. Free teacher guides are available with the videos on request. For any of the above, call the Weather Channel's education department at (770) 801-2503.

The Discovery Channel has free teacher guides available. Call (800) 321-1832.

MTV has a classroom series on social issues entitled Community of the Future and an antiviolence campaign titled Enough is Enough. Monthly lesson plans and video copies of the series are available to teachers. Call (212) 258-8699.

The National Teacher Training Project helps teachers use various technologies including instructional television. Call Sara Feldman at (212) 560-3519.

The Center for Media Literacy offers tools to help children (and adults) to be better viewers and users of media. Call Elizabeth Thoman at (310) 559-2944.

PlayRight is an information resource for teachers and parents that educates them on children's video games. The monthly resource is published by *GamePro*, a video gaming magazine. The cost is $18.00 for six issues. To subscribe, call (800) 238-1313.

Parents' Choice is an information resource on children's media. Published quarterly; a sample copy is available (for $1.50) by writing Parents' Choice, P.O. Box 185, Waban, MA 02168.

The National Media Literacy Project helps integrate media literacy throughout the K–12 curriculum. For further information, call Deirdre Downs at (505) 820-1129.

Cable in the Classroom and Harvard University have a project that aims to teach media literacy to public school students, grades K–12. Call Sharon Metcalf at (703) 845-1400.

Beyond TV: Activities for Using Video with Children contains activities for television in the classroom. For further information, call (800) 422-2546.

discovering the best and most appropriate software for your class, a particular student, or for recommending home use to parents. Each issue has reviews of a dozen new software programs for kids. Criteria include educational value, economic value, simplicity of use, design, and whether or not the program is entertaining and holds child interest.

Ask for: Free sample copy.

Requirements: None. Annual subscription is $24.00.

EDUCATIONAL RESOURCES
(800) 624-2926

■ Offers free CD-ROM that allows you to try software before purchase. Demo includes product information on 140-plus titles.

Ask for: Free CD-ROM.

Requirements: None.

LINDY ENTERPRISES, INC.
(800) 937-8227

■ Offers a free demo disk of their Macintosh-based product. See a sampler of their math assessment program, interactive reading software, various extension activities, mock trials and debates (in which the student is the main character in the story). Printout capability of demo includes product price list and information on disk-based, CD-ROM, or site-license products to bring this technology to every computer in your school.

Ask for: Free demo disk.

Requirements: None.

SMART STUFF & GOOD IDEAS
44-147 Bay View Haven Place
Kaneohe, HI 96744
(800) 207-6278

■ Offers software and board games that reinforce fundamental educational skills. Programs and games run the gamut from age four, through every grade level, to adult. Excellent even for adults going back to school and needing a fundamentals brushup. Special software includes educational software and some bilingual (French and Spanish).

Ask for: Free loaner demo disk (please return within 30 days) and catalog.

Requirements: None.

THE SOFTWARE PLACE

P.O. Box 26688
Austin, TX 78755
(800) 950-8565

■ Provides discounted educational software.

Ask for: A free catalog.

Requirements: Write for catalog; toll-free number is for orders only.

TEACHER SUPPORT SOFTWARE

1035 Northwest 57th Street
Gainesville, FL 32605
(800) 228-2871

■ A company designed and owned by teachers, for teachers. It offers a free demo disk, "Reading Realities," for elementary school students (grades 2–6) and for middle/high school "at risk" students. Also offers *Teacher Support Software,* hard copy, chapter-by-chapter lesson plans, with reproducibles, for $6.50. Markets "Time Saving Tools" software, for $63.00, which includes "Work Sheet Magic" (create worksheets), "Make-A-Flash" (create flash cards), and "Make-A-Book." Software runs on MS-DOS and the Mac (some applications for Apple 2).

Ask for: Free demo disk (state which age group).

Requirements: None.

TEXAS INSTRUMENTS

P.O. Box 6118
Temple, TX 76503-6102
(800) TICARES

■ Texas Instruments (TI) makes instructional product lines, namely a series of calculators developed with help from educators to support the full gamut of education from kindergarten through graduate school and into professional life! Hence, TI

Your Local Cable Company Has a Great Deal for You

Cable's commitment is to donate and install one or two lines into a library, classroom, or computer lab. If you need the entire school cabled (or, upgraded, as the case may be), they ask that you encourage your principal to seek school district approval for the job. If cable is put in a budget, TCI will do bids, design, etc. But, regardless, two lines are free.

Cable also purchases up to five *Cable in the Classroom* magazines per school. The magazines are then mailed directly from the publisher to the teacher or school who requests them. The subscription has no time limit, so you could get a free magazine for years to come!

Cable is making some bold fund-raising experiments. They have fund-raisers wherein they match funds for every dollar a customer donates to schools. They will often donate VCRs and other equipment.

Special offers, such as teacher workshops, are often available on a limited time offer.

So call your local cable company and see what unbelievably good deals are available right now.

starts a relationship with its future customers early, and is interested in helping teachers teach through its technology.

TI offers teachers' kits and workshops to help teachers and students alike learn the technology of the calculator and various programming devices. Their free newsletters—*80 Something* and *TICARES*—are available to help the learning process. TI also has a toll-free line to help educators with technology questions.

Ask for: *80 Something, TICARES,* TI81 Programming Package.

Requirements: None

Chapter Nine

Global Awareness

 Learning about the differences and similarities among us creates tolerance and empathy for all peoples of this world. This section is for those who have made the commitment to reflect cultural diversity in their classrooms.

Tips for promoting multicultural awareness in the classroom:

- Understand others; support equality and human rights.
- Study history for understanding. Look beyond stereotypes.
- Learn about ethnic groups' holidays.
- Read books on others' cultural background as well as your own.

Multicultural Activities

The classroom is a great place to create cross-cultural experiences where students from diverse backgrounds learn about each other. Try these activities.

- Create your own "culture" for a week. Create real, "being there" activities. Study a culture—its foods, thoughts, and customs. Make artifacts, listen to its music, sing, and wear the clothing of the culture. Become the culture.

- Try the cooking of various cultures as a hands-on student activity. To help you get started, we recommend *All Around the World Cookbook* by Sheila Lukins, Workman Publishing Co. (See Chapter 2 for Workman's address and telephone number.)
- Research *Chase's Calendar of Annual Events* for listings of various international activities celebrated throughout the year.
- Take a field trip to local arts venues that sponsor programs that represent ethnic diversity.
- Create your own multicultural fair at school!
- Organize a multicultural arts and music festival.
- Write a report on an international organization working for human rights, social justice, world hunger, environmental concerns, world peace.

Discovering the Real World Through Music

Discover the music of the world from the Real World record label, the brainchild of rock and world-beat legend Peter Gabriel. The record label began with the release of a Peter Gabriel soundtrack and grew into a label of some fifty plus albums (and counting) of Third World and international artists.

The music is heard worldwide—by up to 100,000 people at a time—via the World in the Park organization's World of Music Art and Dance (WOMAD). Real World and WOMAD have considerable credibility because Gabriel helps and promotes (instead of exploiting) Third World artists. Quoting Real World's magazine, *The Box*, on their "Exploring the Music of the World" resource packs:

> A new series of comprehensive resource packs to support any music or social studies course. Each pack introduces students to the distinctive melodies and rhythms of the region. The packs are ring bound containing: two cassettes of musical excerpts for performing and listening work, detailed teachers' notes and project sheets for students, and a full-color poster providing background information on the culture surrounding the music. As was reported in *Times Educational Supplement*, teachers and students who have taken part in piloting the materials have been enthusiastic about it. Proceeds to WOMAD Foundation.

The two packs available:

- WBK2, Music of West Africa
- WBK2, Music of the Caribbean

Check out not only these Teachers' Packages but also the entire Real World label (found in the back of *The Box*). *The Box* is an excellent source of information on human rights (Gabriel has performed benefit concerts for Amnesty International and is a known advocate for political prisoners' rights) and various essays on all matters global, including the ozone layer, political oppression, state-of-the-art technology, future vision, and the problems of Tibet.

THE BOX
P.O. Box 35
Bath, Avon BA1 1YJ
England
+44 225 744464; fax: +44 225 743481

Harrambe: Bringing Community-Based Conservation to the Shambas of Africa from the Neighborhoods of America.

The Harrambe project* aims to create wildlife club start-up kits to bring grassroots conservation projects to schools, clubs, and families.

WHAT IS HARRAMBE?

"Harrambe" in Swahili means "pulling together." In the Harrambe Project, communities in Kenya and America pull together for the sake of their children, Earth, and its wildlife—particularly African elephants.

The pilot Harrambe project began in 1986 with a small group of California kids and their families who wanted to help

---

*This information graciously provided by, and reprinted from, Nilgiri Press. Note that this project can tie into not only global awareness but any science or environmental unit.

elephants. Calling themselves Friends of Wildlife or FOWL, they contacted Dr. David Western, a conservation biologist, now director of the Kenya Wildlife Service.

Dr. Western told FOWL about a Masai village outside Amboseli Park, Kenya, where 60 elephants had been speared that year. Why? The elephants raided and destroyed Masai crops, and the villagers in turn were forced to spear many elephants in self-defense. Would the kids help?

"Yes!" FOWL set out to educate themselves and their community about the elephants and people of the Amoseli region of Kenya. They earned money to pay for a solar electric fence to protect Masai crops from raiding elephants. This campaign called for working and pulling together in harmony.

Meanwhile, the Masai farmers and their families set out to build the fence and to learn to maintain it. This parallel campaign in Kenya meant working hard and pulling together in harmony, too.

With the fence completed in 1990, crop-raiding stopped. In the last five years, the elephants—no longer tempted by easy snacks and safe from poaching—have spread out from the overcrowded park and returned to their ancient migration routes. Soon the overgrazed parklands will begin to recover.

As for the Masai, their crops are safe. They have excess corn to sell, and they have used profits to build a school. Learning to work hard and pull together has restored strong community bonds.

When FOWL started the Harrambe project, the kids thought they would help elephants and a Masai community. Only later did they realize that Harrambe helped them too. When people pull together in harmony for a noble cause, they develop deeper friendships, parents and children grow closer, their community grows stronger, and everyone realizes that "pulling together" can be a lot of fun.

With your help, communities in Africa and America can pull together for the sake of their children, Earth, and its wild African elephants. Harrambe is setting up a revolving fund, through the Wildlife Conservation Society in New York, for which American groups can raise money in the Harrambe fashion. Then, Masai villages can borrow funds to fence in their small farms. Upon repayment, other villages can borrow the funds for yet more fencing.

WHY IS HARRAMBE SPECIAL?

- One hundred percent of your money goes directly toward buying materials for a village's protective fence.
- Masai people work together to help themselves, without "outside experts."
- The amount of your contribution is not as important as your spirit of Harrambe—pulling together with family and friends.
- Harrambe is not charity. A village borrows money knowing that its repayment gives the next village a chance.
- Villagers now benefit by protecting elephants, rather than killing them.
- The fences encourage the elephants to return to their traditional migration routes.

HOW CAN I HELP THE HARRAMBE PROJECT?

There are two ways to help: Raise awareness and raise funds.

We can raise awareness so that others become involved in the Harrambe Project. We can raise funds for constructing solar-powered fences in Kenya, an undertaking of proven long-range benefit to both the elephants and the Masai.

Raising Awareness

Step one involves informing yourself.

Read all you can about elephants, community-based conservation, the Masai, and Kenya. Recommended reading includes:

Elephant Memories by Cynthia Moss

Growing Up Masai by Tom Shachtman

The Land and People of Kenya by Michael Maren

Take Your Time, Your Life Is Your Message, and
  The Compassionate Universe by Eknath Easwaran

Encourage students to take advantage of school programs to learn more, to sign up for relevant courses—ecology, anthropology—and to choose report topics that allow them to understand more fully the people and wildlife of the Amboseli ecosystem.

Step two involves informing others.

Write letters to your local newspapers and magazines, encouraging readers to join Harrambe. Write Nilgiri Press, P.O. Box 256, Tomales, California 94971, for information that you can copy and distribute on Harrambe.

Encourage students to talk to family, friends, neighbors, and classmates. As a teacher, talk to your peers. Let students present oral reports, skits, puppet shows, and create displays or slide shows. Take advantage of local environmental fairs. The organizations at Nilgiri, Earthforce and FOWL, can help with ideas on how to become involved with environmental fairs—call (707) 878-2369.

Raising Funds

Step one involves simplifying your life.

Resist the impulse to buy something you don't need or to eat something your body doesn't need. Then, save the money you would have spent and contribute it to the Harrambe fund.

Step two involves organizing fund-raising events.

Whenever you collect money from other people it is important to tell them exactly how the funds will be used and assure them that all proceeds will go directly to the Harrambe Project. Here are some fund-raising ideas that Earthforce has used:

1. Washing cars
2. Polishing shoes
3. Holding bake sales
4. Selling T-shirts, posters, buttons
5. Making and selling greeting cards
6. Putting on a benefit play or concert

Make a tax-deductible donation payable to: Wildlife Conservation Society, International Programs, Bronx, NY 10460. Be sure to write "Harrambe Fund" on your check and on the front of your envelope.

Multicultural Resources

CHURCH WORLD SERVICE OFFICE OF GLOBAL EDUCATION

P.O. Box 968
Elkhart, IN 46515
(219) 264-3102

■ Free lending library of films, including children's educational films.

Ask for: Catalog.
Requirements: None.

CLASSROOM TODAY

(800) 321-3106

■ This biannual newspaper was developed to encourage growing readers, often with stories of American ethnic diversity.

Ask for: Free copy of *Classroom Today.*
Requirements: None.

OXFAM AMERICA

115 Broadway
Boston, MA 02116
(617) 482-1211

■ Produces the Third World Calendar, a photographic collection portraying people in developing countries.

Ask for: Information.
Requirements: None.

PBS VIDEO

1320 Braddock Place
Alexandria, VA 22314
(703) 739-5000

■ Check with your local, city, or school library (or any of the Internet educational resources described within this book) for suggestions on books, audiocassettes, and videotapes about various cultures and their history.

Ask for: Listing of videos.

Requirements: None.

PLAN INTERNATIONAL USA
155 Plan Way
Warwick, RI 02886
(401) 738-5600

■ Videotapes and slides available on loan.

Ask for: Catalog.

Requirements: None.

SKIPPING STONES
P.O. Box 3939
Eugene, OR 97403-0939
(503) 342-4956

■ A multicultural journal that is a window on the world for children. A great way to show life experiences of children throughout the world. Emphasizes cooperation among students the world over. Sections include a parents' guide, a teacher's guide, and a book list that can help you start a multicultural library.

Ask for: Skipping Stones.

Requirements: $18.00 for a bimonthly subscription.

SYRACUSE CULTURAL WORKERS
Attn: Linda Malik, Art Director
P.O. Box 6367
Syracuse, NY 13217
(315) 474-1132

■ Produces a "Peace Calendar," a celebration of multicultural diversity, that lists holidays and historical dates from many ethnic groups. Other resources include holiday cards (for seasonal holidays such as Chanukah, Solstice). Their mission is "To empower individuals to achieve and celebrate social and environmental justice by providing a vision of a progressive culture." Their message is stated clearly on the calendar itself: "Lasting peace can only be achieved by creating a climate of justice in which freedom, economic equality, and respect for all living beings can flourish."

Ask for: Information.

Requirements: None.

TWIN SISTERS PRODUCTIONS
1340 Home Avenue, Suite D
Akron, OH 44310
(216) 929-0070

■ Help your students learn Spanish, German, French, or Italian—or learn a new language yourself. Audiocassettes introduce simple words and phrases set to sing-along songs. Includes an illustrated learning guide. Designed for bilingual use: English on one side and the foreign language on the reverse. Thus foreign students can learn English in the same manner.

Ask for: Free study guide.

Requirements: Send a business-size self-addressed, stamped envelope (SASE) or $9.98 for a 60-minute cassette and learning guide.

UNITED NATIONS CHILDREN'S FUND (UNICEF)
886 United Nations Plaza
New York, NY 10017
(212) 326-7000

■ Free lending library of films, tapes, publications, and slides.

Ask for: Information.

Requirements: None.

Helping UNICEF While UNICEF Helps You

UNICEF has been a top supporter of multicultural education. Past campaigns have included "Global Awareness in the Classroom: Africa—Focus on the Environment," in which a teaching guide and poster helped students learn about the people and natural resources of this region. UNICEF also shares excellent fund-raising ideas. Don't forget the traditional orange Halloween collection cartons, which help others in need.

UNITED FARM WORKERS
Box 62
Keene, CA 93531
(805) 822-5571

■ Offers free videotape on the history of the grape boycott.

Ask for: No Grapes.
Requirements: None.

Book and Audio Publishers

AUDIO PARTNERS PUBLISHING CORP.
1133 High Street
P.O. Box 6930
Auburn, CA 95604
(916) 888-7803; fax (916) 888-7805

■ Offers a special unabridged cassette inspiring moral vision in coping with the contemporary racial crisis in America: *Race Matters* by Cornel West, professor at the Harvard University Divinity School and Harvard's Department of Afro-American Studies. The *New York Times* bestseller, now on audiocassette, "resonates with the power of West's voice and views."

Ask for: Information about *Race Matters* and other audiotapes.

Requirements: Call (800) 231-4261 to order.

CHARLESBRIDGE PUBLISHING
85 Main Street
Watertown, MA 02172-4411
(617) 926-0329

■ Offers thematic resources for the integrated classroom: whole-language books, critical thinking, multicultural children's literature, and Spanish and bilingual reading, math, and literature.

Ask for: Multicultural catalog.

Requirements: None.

JOHN MUIR PUBLICATIONS
P.O. Box 613
Santa Fe, NM 87504
(505) 982-4078

■ Publishes books on multicultural themes, parenting, environmental studies, and science. Multicultural lines include:

- American Origins Series: *Tracing Our English Roots*, *Tracing Our Chinese Roots*, etc.
- Kids Explore Series: *Kids Explore America's African-American Heritage*, *Kids Explore America's Hispanic Heritage*, and *Kids Explore America's Japanese-American Heritage*
- Rainbow Warrior Artists Series: *Native Artists of Africa*, *Native Artists of Europe*, and *Native Artists of North America*

The Rainbow Warrior Artists Series can be used across the curriculum in art (as it explores creativity exercises) and environment studies (for it shows a culture living in harmony with the Earth).

Ask for: Multicultural catalog.

Requirements: None.

"Strategies for Teaching Critical Thinking Across the Curriculum"

Charlesbridge Publishing in association with Educational Testing Service has developed this four-day professional seminar. Its theme is "Make thinking across the curriculum a reality in every classroom." To bring this seminar to your district, call (800) 225-3214.

MILLIKEN PUBLISHING COMPANY
1100 Research Boulevard
P.O. Box 21579
St. Louis, MO 63132
(314) 991-4220; (800) 325-4126

■ An excellent source of resource guides, diagrammatic study prints, and workbooks. Publishes reproducible books on history, an art and culture series, and a series called *Cultural Fair,* which offers step-by-step instructions on developing a multicultural unit—from choosing a social studies topic through displaying projects at a cultural fair.

Ask for: Multicultural catalog.

Requirements: None.

STEMMER HOUSE PUBLISHERS, INC.
2627 Caves Road
Owings Mills, MD 21117
(410) 363-3690

■ Stemmer is a publishing house of an "eighteenth century vintage." Their multicultural list includes a retelling of the Finnish epic *Kalevala* and the International Design Library, which gathers together designs of cultures throughout the world, including

Native American, African, and Celtic designs. The International Design Library "has been created to offer artists, designers, craftspeople, and students of art history a library of idea sourcebooks that are filled with usable copyright-free art and inspiration for graphic treatments, craft designs, interior and exterior decoration, and documentation of authentic design styles, periods, and ethnic groups. Each book is 8½" × 11", 48 or 56 pages, paperbound."

Ask for: Multicultural catalog.

Requirements: None.

SUNDANCE
Publishers & Distributors
550 Newton Road
P.O. Box 1326
Littleton, MA 01460
(800) 343-8204

■ A great source for instructional materials PreK–12. Of particular interest is their "Multicultural Big Book Calendar Program," which features a perpetual calendar that *never* goes out-of-date because *you* fill in the numbers. Program features include:

- Multicultural Big Books: help introduce various cultures
- Teacher's Big Book Classroom Calendar: designed with beautiful multicultural art; also serves as your monthly planner
- Take-Home Student Calendar: replicates the Classroom Calendar in a smaller format and includes questions for parents and children to encourage discussion of multicultural themes.

Ask for: Multicultural catalog.

Requirements: None.

URBAN EDUCATION (UD)

Teachers College, Columbia University
Institute for Urban and Minority Education
Main Hall, Room 303, Box 40
525 West 120th Street
New York, NY 10027-9998
(800) 601-4868 or (212) 678-3433; fax: (212) 678-4048;
E-mail: eric-cue@columbia.edu

■ Offers various information alerts and resources on information on urban schools, education strategies to combat racism, and creating a bias-free environment for young children. Will send a full list of publications with prices for the monographs. Single copies of the digests and information alerts are free with SASE.

   Microfiche or paper copies available from the ERIC Document Reproduction Service, 3900 Wheeler Avenue, Alexandria, VA 22304-6409, (800) 227-ERIC.

Ask for: Informational brochures.

Requirements: Send a business-size SASE.

WILLIAM MORROW & COMPANY

1350 Avenue of the Americas
New York, NY 10019
(212) 261-6792

■ Many of Morrow's imprints publish books on cultural diversity. The categories are broken down in ethnic groups from the Americas, Europe, the Commonwealth of Independent States, Africa, Middle East, Asia, Australia, and Greenland. They also offer books of Jewish interest, multiethnic images, and international perspective and books in foreign languages.

Ask for: Multicultural catalog.

Requirements: None.

Hate Hotline—Call (800) 347-HATE

The most dangerous weapon on Earth is ignorance.
Educate for understanding.
Teach tolerance.

If you have been victimized by, witnessed, or have information about a community conflict based on hate, race, or national origin—or if you are aware of rising racial tensions in your community—call the 24-hour, toll-free, hate hotline. The hotline is a part of the Community Relations Service (CRS) of the U.S. Department of Justice.

Multicultural History Months

AFRICAN-AMERICAN HISTORY MONTH
(February)
Lianna Miles, Managing Director
Associated Publishers
1407 14th Street, NW
Washington DC, 20005
(202) 265-1441

■ Starts the last Friday of January

Ask for: Further information.

Requirements: None.

NATIONAL HISPANIC HERITAGE MONTH
(September 15–October 15)
Viva California
Gamut Promotions and Advertising
1132 North Hunter
Stockton, CA 95202
(209) 466-6658

Ask for: Further information.

Requirements: None.

NATIONAL WOMEN'S HISTORY MONTH
(March)
National Women's History Project
7738 Bell Road
Windsor, CA 95492
(707) 838-6000

Ask for: Further information.

Requirements: None.

Human Rights Organizations

AMNESTY INTERNATIONAL USA (AIUSA)
322 8th Avenue
New York, NY 10001
(212) 207-8400

INSTITUTE FOR GLOBAL COMMUNICATIONS NETWORKS
18 De Boom Street
San Francisco, CA 94107
(415) 442-0220

■ A nonprofit organization providing computer networking and communications consulting services to people interested in environmental protection, sustainable development, human rights, social justice, and peace. Networks include PeaceNet, Conflict-Net, and EcoNet. Accessible with computer and modem. Offers Internet access, e-mail, and electronic methods to contact world leaders.

UNITED NATIONS (UN)
886 United Nations Plaza
New York, NY 10017
(212) 963-1234 or (212) 963-4475

■ You can write the UN for listings of embassies, which will provide maps and brochures that students can use in nation research projects. Letters sent to embassies should be addressed to Information Officer. Also offers an information package designed to assist teachers in teaching about the UN. It contains three categories of materials: general background information, information on how to obtain further educational resources, and additional publications of interest.

The scope of the UN has broadened in recent years, and programs for the environment, economic and social development, eliminating racial discrimination, and promoting respect for human rights have expanded to reach more parts of the globe. Of interest to teachers:

- *United Nations Family: A Selected Bibliography*: an annotated list of basic publications of the UN and its related agencies
- *Basic Facts About the United Nations*: standard reference book
- *Everyone's United Nations*: standard reference book
- *World Concerns and the United Nations: Model Teaching Units for Primary, Secondary and Teacher Education*: when organizing your curriculum and developing themes on the UN, you may wish to consult this book as a guide (available from the UN Publications, Room DC2-0853, for $12.00—sales number E.86.I.8).

Chapter Ten

Teacher Education and Professional Development

 Teachers must continually educate themselves if they are to educate others. Teacher education and professional development should be a right, not a luxury.

The other chapters in this book provide contacts and ideas to help you save time and money—all with your students in mind. This chapter provides information that also benefits you, the teacher, in professional development. It also encourages you to remain on the edge of progressive thinking. And it advocates that a teacher is not "merely" a teacher of his or her students, but is also a community resource.

As a professional, you will find your sphere of influence extends beyond your students. How can your efforts be reinforced at your students' homes? What if the problems you have in the classroom stem from difficulties at home? What if the parents need education referrals (in everything from learning ESL to learning conflict management to learning personal growth)? Well, this chapter also suggests ways teachers, parents, and the community can help students. The issues covered range from helping a child learn to read, to referring parents to educational resources, to using conflict resolution to handle emergencies such as gang problems and drugs.

Travel Opportunities

COUNCIL ON INTERNATIONAL EDUCATIONAL EXCHANGE (CIEE)
205 East 42nd Street
New York, NY 10017-5706
(212) 661-1414, ext. 1108; telex: 423227/6730395;
fax: (212) 972-3231
Cable: Costudents

■ Publishes *Travel Options: For Educators,* a free annual publication that features opportunities and advantages available to teachers when they travel. This essential guide contains information on everything from obtaining educator discounts on airfares to participating in international exchanges with educators from all over the world.

Whether teaching at the elementary, secondary, undergraduate, or graduate level, and whether traveling with students, fellow educators, or independently, a variety of programs and services are available exclusively to educators. For instance, the International Teacher Identity Card opens the door for travel discounts to educators. Opportunities are also available for teachers to study the education systems of the United Kingdom and France or to be part of the groups of educators from around the world who are gathering at prestigious international universities to explore the changes in our global community.

These and many other opportunities are outlined in *Travel Options.*

Ask for: Free copy of *Travel Options: For Educators.*

Requirements: None.

EARTHWATCH
680 Mt. Auburn Street
P.O. Box 403
Watertown, MA 02272
(617) 926-8200; fax: (617) 926-8532;
Internet: info@earthwatch.org

■ Encompasses a wide range of scientific disciplines and addresses numerous environmental issues. Offers teachers (and other members of the public) unique opportunities to work side-by-side with field scientists and scholars. Their mission is "to improve human understanding of the planet, the diversity of its inhabitants, and the processes that affect the quality of life on Earth."

For teachers, this is an opportunity to obtain some immeasurable hands-on science experience and professional education. Some expeditions by subject matter are listed here.

• Understanding the Earth: projects include atmospheric science, climatology, geology, glaciology, global change, hydrology, paleontology, soil science, and volcanology.

• Helping Threatened Habitats: projects include biodiversity, botany, conservation biology, entomology, evolutionary biology, herpetology, mammalogy, mariculture, reef management, and wetland ecology.

• Strategies for Living: projects include adaptation, animal communication, botany, conservation biology, evolution, land use, marine mammalogy, nutrition, physiology, ornithology, primatology, social behavior, and wildlife management.

• Human Impacts: projects include alternative energy, anatomy, anthropology, architecture, archaeology, art history, cartography, civil engineering, cultural evolution, economics, ethnobotany, folklore, history, land use, maternal nutrition, metallurgy, paleoanthropology, public health, social work, and sustainable living.

• Managing the Planet: projects including animal behavior, animal husbandry, geography, engineering, environmental planning, forensics, forestry, horticulture, land reclamation,

Information on The Council on International Exchange

The Council on International Exchange, established in 1947, is a worldwide nonprofit organization dedicated to developing and supporting international educational exchange as a means to build understanding and peaceful cooperation among peoples of the world. With a membership of more than 250 educational institutions, it administers a variety of study, work, and travel programs for students and educators in 33 countries on six continents, and operates an international network of travel services.

meteorology, ornithology, predator ecology, soil science, sustainable development, and wildlife and wetland management.

Contact Earthwatch for further information on expeditions, membership, EarthCorps bulletin, teacher/student fellowships.

Ask for: Basic information for interested teachers.

Requirements: None.

EPCOT TEACHER'S PASS
(407) 824-4321 or (407) 560-7277

■ Allows teachers the opportunity to experience the educational resources of Disney's Epcot in Florida. Teachers can visit the Epcot outreach center, where they will find lesson plans and other resources.

Ask for: Information about Epcot Teacher's Pass.

Requirements: Must present Epcot Guest Relations with a copy of your active teaching credentials, verification of current employment via a letter on school letterhead signed by school administrator, and photo identification.

OVERSEAS VACATION
Center for International Education
Fulbright-Hays Seminars Abroad Program
U.S. Department of Education
600 Independence Avenue, SW
Washington, DC 20202-5332
(202) 732-6061

■ Offers summer seminars for humanities and social sciences educators.

Ask for: Application information and a list of available seminars.

Requirements: Fourth grade through postsecondary teachers.

STUDY A LANGUAGE ABROAD
NEH Fellowship Program for Foreign Language Teachers K–12
Connecticut College
270 Mohegan Avenue
New London, CT 06320
(203) 439-2282

■ Offers elementary and secondary school teachers opportunity to obtain a fellowship for six weeks of summer study abroad.

Ask for: Application information.

Requirements: For foreign language educators.

TEACH OVERSEAS
Department of Defense Dependents Schools
Teacher-Recruitment Section
4040 North Fairfax Drive
Arlington, VA 22203-1634
(703) 696-3068

■ The U.S. Department of Defense provides an opportunity to teach children of military and Defense Department civilian personnel abroad.

Ask for: Application and information.

Requirements: For elementary and secondary school teachers.

TEACHER EXCHANGE PROGRAM
Fulbright Teacher Program
600 Maryland Avenue, SW, Room 142
Washington, DC 20024-2520
(800) 726-0479

■ Provides opportunities for classroom-to-classroom teacher exchanges between American teachers and their counterparts from various countries around the world.

Ask for: Application and guidelines.

Requirements: Stated in guidelines.

WORLD LEARNING INC.
Kipling Road
P.O. Box 676
Brattleboro, VT 05302-0676
(802) 257-7751; fax: (802) 258-3248

■ Founded in 1932 as the U.S. Experiment in International Living, World Learning has sustained its founding concept—*learning the culture and language of another country by living as a member of one of its families*—while pioneering new initiatives in response to a changing world. Its mission is to enable participants to develop the knowledge, skills, and attitudes needed to contribute effectively to international understanding and global development.

Resources can be found in two areas. One is the Professional Development and Resource Center (PDRC). They publish a free newsletter listing jobs in the education and international fields. Call or write PDRC at the main address—Attn: Tony Drapelick, Box GD, (802) 258-3396; fax: (802) 258-3248.

They also have additional resources to assist with job location and development. The second area is general program information. For information regarding the fourteen programs listed here, call or write the main address—Attn: Janet Meynell, Box GD, (802) 258-3170; fax: (802) 258-3136.

The fourteen programs are:

- Masters of Arts in Teaching Program: prepares language teachers committed to professional development and service in their field. Participants concentrate in French, Spanish, or English to speakers of other languages.
- Master's Program in Intercultural Management: this graduate program provides competency-based, professional-level training for intercultural managers. Participants concentrate on sustainable development, international education, or training and human resource development.
- Bachelor's Program in World Issues: a two year, upper-division bachelor's program offering a degree in international studies. Participants concentrate on at least one of these areas: peace, social and economic development, and environment.
- College Semester Abroad: administers more than 50 study abroad programs in more than 35 countries in every part of the world for college and university students.
- Summer Abroad: offers high school students homestays, travel, language training, ecological adventure, and community service in Africa, Asia, Australia, Europe, and Latin America.
- Elderhostel™: international homestay and education programs for participants aged 60 years and older, offered in cooperation with Elderhostel, Inc.
- Homestay/USA: welcomes international participants, aged 13 to over 80, into U.S. homes for several days, weeks, or months.
- International High School Program/Congress-Bundestag Youth Exchange Program: traditional exchange program where 15–18-year-old students from around the world stay with volunteer host families and attend public high schools for an academic year or a semester in the United States. U.S. students enjoy a similar program in Germany.
- *Au Pair* Homestay: offers a practical solution to child care for U.S. families and a cost-effective way for European *au pairs* to work and study in the United States for a year. A similar reciprocal program is offered for U.S. *au pairs* and host families in several European countries.

- International Students of English: intensive English language training program for college-age and older students, featuring small, four-week classes on U.S. campuses.
- Executive English Programs: intensive language and cross-cultural training for business and professional clients, tailored to the global marketplace and custom-designed to meet the needs of the individual, small group, or entire company.
- Youth Adventure Camp: ideal blend of language training, recreation, and cultural discovery for 11–15-year-old students from around the world.
- Development Management: supports projects that help local public and private institutions promote social and economic change through on-the-job training and workshops.
- Human Resources Development: supports projects that help increase the capacities of individuals to secure employment, play dynamic roles in their chosen fields, and contribute to the communities in which they live.

Ask for: Free newsletter and information.

Requirements: None.

Publications and Videos

ACADEMIC THERAPY PUBLICATIONS
High Noon Books
Ann Arbor Division
20 Commercial Boulevard
Novato, CA 94949-6191
(415) 883-3314 or (800) 422-7249 (outside California)

■ Offers several teacher/parent resources, including *Helpmates: 35 Brochures for Teachers to Share with Parents,* which costs $10.00 and contains 35 reproducible brochures. "For Your Information" brochures help parents learn to do a better job, not by criticizing but by showing that people care and are interested in establishing a mutual dialogue for the children's sake. The information is published in English and similar information is often available in Spanish. The brochures are also rich in further reading suggestions. Titles include:

- "Helping Your Child at Home with Reading"
- "Helping Your Child at Home with Arithmetic"
- "Helping Your Child at Home with Spelling"
- "Helping Your Child at Home with Handwriting"
- "Helping Your Child at Home with Vocabulary"
- "Helping Your Child at Home with Geography"
- "Helping Your Child with Creative Writing Assignments"
- "Reading Comprehension Activities in the Home"
- "Using Newspapers, Periodicals, and Other Resources to Help Your Child with Reading"
- "Helping Your Child at Home with the Neurological Impress Method of Reading"
- "Helping Your Child with General Study Tips"
- "Helping Your Child with Homework"
- "Helping Your Child Overcome Spatial Problems"
- "Helping Your Child Prepare for the Holidays"
- "Holiday Reading for Families"
- "Preparing for a School Conference"
- "Establishing a Parent-Teacher Relationship"
- "Safeguard Those Valuable Papers"
- "Helping Your Child Get Ready to Take a Trip"
- "Helping Your Child with Socialization"
- "Helping Parents with Their Child's Physical Development"
- "Sex Education: A Reading List for Parents"
- "Dealing with Substance Abuse: A Reference List for Parents and Teachers"
- "The Parent Is the Child's First Teacher"
- "Dear Parent"
- "Preparing for a Disaster"
- "Helping a Parent with Sibling Rivalry"

- "Helping Your Child Develop Self-Esteem"
- "Helping Your Child Deal with His Fears"
- "Dealing with Discipline"
- "Television and Children"
- "Choosing a Baby Sitter"
- "Basic Terms in Learning"
- "A Few Words on Nutrition"
- "Parents Rights Under the New Law"

Ask for: Helpmates.

Requirements: $10.00.

ACHIEVEMENT, INC.

485 South Broadway, Suite 12
Hicksville, NY 11801
(516) 931-2500 or (800) 645-8989; fax: (516) 931-2575

■ A division of Focus Media, Inc., an educational publisher of audiovisuals and computer software. Their ongoing line of audio products is designed to "help parents deal with real-life problems."

Ask for: New catalog/information sheets.

Requirements: Tapes are approximately $8.00 each.

BARBARA BUSH FOUNDATION FOR FAMILY LITERACY

1002 Wisconsin Avenue, NW
Washington, DC 20007
(202) 338-2006

■ Offers *Barbara Bush's Family Reading Tips* free of charge and *First Teachers: A Family Literacy Handbook for Parents, Policy Makers, and Literacy Providers* for $4.00.

Ask for: Ordering information.

Requirements: None, except price noted above.

THE BEAVERS
HCR 70, Box 537
La Porte, MN 56461
(218) 224-2182

■ Publishes *Travel Games,* a popular resource for children that has sold more than a half million copies, and sells for the modest price of $1.50 to cover shipping and handling costs. The orders are mailed by bulk so it may take three to four weeks for delivery.

Ask for: Travel Games.

Requirements: None.

BLOCKBUSTER ENTERTAINMENT
One Blockbuster Plaza
Fort Lauderdale, FL 33301-1860
(305) 832-3250; fax: (305) 832-3920

■ Did you know that you can get a free rental in almost any video shop of the Magic Johnson and Arsenio Hall video *Time Out: The Truth About HIV, AIDS, and You* and the conflict management/gun prevention special television report *Kids Killing Kids?*

Check your local video store to see what free community services videos they have. For instance, Blockbuster Entertainment carries 287 free videos on everything from nutrition to fire safety to doing taxes! Not all of the 287 videos are in any one store, but they are all located in the main computer for potential special order. Go to your local store and browse the Community Services section.

Ask for: Community Services Videos sheet.

Requirements: None

CAROUSEL PRESS

P.O. Box 6061
Albany, CA 94706-0061
(510) 527-5849

■ Offers free 1998 edition of the 32-page *Family Travel Guides Catalogue* to help you, your students, or your students' parents plan an educational vacation. (Send $1.00 postage or a business-size SASE with 2-oz. first-class postage.) Other guide books include:

- *Miles of Smiles: 101 Great Car Games and Activities*
- *San Francisco Family Fun*
- *Weekend Adventures for City-Weary People: Overnight Trips in Northern California*
- *How to Organize a Babysitting Cooperative and Get Some Free Time Away from the Kids*
- *The Zoo Book: Fun at America's Zoos*

Ask for: Catalog.
Requirements: None.

COMMUNITY UPDATE

(800) USA-LEARN

■ Stay abreast of changes in national education with this free monthly newsletter. Discover how you can join in national satellite town meetings, contribute to a community exchange column, and learn about resources available from the Department of Education, the government, and private companies.

Ask for: Free newsletter.
Requirements: None.

COUNCIL FOR BASIC EDUCATION (CBE)

1319 F Street, NW, Suite 900
Washington, DC 20004-1152
(202) 347-4171; fax: (202) 347-5047

■ CBE was founded by a group of educators who were dismayed at the decline of the intellectual quality of American education.

CBE believes that the basic subjects—English, geography, government, history, mathematics, science, languages, and the arts—provide the basis for a comprehensive education and encourage lifelong learning.

It is comprised of academic, corporate, civic, and philanthropic leaders ". . . devoted to the principle of universal, tax-supported, democratic education." It believes that "only by the maintenance of high academic standards can the idea of democratic education be realized—the ideal of offering to all the children of all the people of the United States not merely an opportunity to attend school, but the privilege of receiving there the soundest education that is afforded any place in the world."

A respected presence in educational reform, CBE's advocacy includes periodicals, books, and public appearances.

Ask for: General information and publications list.

Requirements: None. Some low-cost publications ranging from $2.00 to $20.00 plus $3.00 postage/handling (with special bulk order discounts).

EDUCATORS PROGRESS SERVICE, INC.
214 Center Street
Randolph, WI 53956-1408
(414) 326-3126; fax: (414) 326-3127

■ Provides information about directories of free materials that are yours for the price of the directory that lists them. They stretch across the curriculum but are listed in each directory under Teacher Education and Professional Development.

- "Educators Guide to Free Teaching Aids": free printed materials for elementary and middle school level, $45.00/copy.
- "Educators Guide to Free Filmstrips": free/loan filmstrips, slides, audiotapes, and records, $24.00/copy.
- "Educators Guide to Free Guidance Materials": free/loan filmstrips, slides, tapes, records, and printed materials on guidance, $28.00/copy.
- "Educators Guide to Free Health, Physical Education, and

Recreation Materials": free/loan filmstrips, slides, tapes, records, and printed materials on health, physical education, and recreation, $28.00/copy.

- "Educators Guide to Free Science Materials": free/loan filmstrips, slides, tapes, records, and printed materials on science, $27.00/copy.

- "Educators Guide to Free Social Studies Materials": free/loan filmstrips, slides, tapes, records, and printed materials on social studies, $29.00/copy.

- "Educators Guide to Free Videotapes": free/loan videotapes, $26.00/copy.

- "Educators Index to Free Materials": free printed materials for high school and college.

Ask for: Ordering information.

Requirements: None

INTERNATIONAL READING ASSOCIATION (IRA)
800 Barksdale Road
P.O. Box 8139
Newark, DE 19714-8139
(800) 336-READ or (302) 731-1600

■ The IRA (listed in fuller detail in Chapter 2), offers a large selection of materials for parents and teachers who are interested in helping young people to read. These materials can also be helpful in bridging a gap between teacher and child, or teacher and parent, or child and parent. Samples of these brochures (some available in English, French, and Spanish) include:

- "Your Home is Your Child's First School"
- "You Can Encourage Your Child to Read"
- "Good Books Make Reading Fun for Your Child"
- "Summer Reading Is Important"
- "You Can Use Television to Stimulate Your Child's Reading Habits"
- "Studying: A Key to Success—Ways Parents Can Help"

- "You Can Help Your Child in Reading Using the Newspaper"
- "Eating Well Can Help Your Child Learn Better"
- "You Can Prepare Your Child for Reading Tests"
- "You Can Help Your Child Connect Reading to Writing"
- "Literacy Development and Early Childhood"
- "Favorite Paperbacks"

Ask for: Membership information and catalog of publications.

Requirements: Fees vary—some free brochures available.

LIBERTY FINANCIAL
(800) 403-KIDS

■ Offers free booklet designed for parents, titled the *Liberty Financial Young Investor Parents' Guide*. Booklet can be adapted for classroom use for lessons in math, cost of living, financial planning, and more.

Ask for: Free booklet.

Requirements: None.

MODERN TALKING PICTURE SERVICE, INC.
5000 Park Street North
St. Petersburg, FL 33709
(800) 243-6877; fax: (800) 237-7143

■ Offers free loan videos (for a five-day viewing period), films (one-day viewing period), and teaching materials on: agriculture, business and economics, driver's education, fine arts, flying and aviation safety, general interest, home economics, medical/health sciences, safety, religion and philosophy, science, and social studies. Programs are loaned free of charge and are returned via the postage-paid return label enclosed with the program. Formats range from VHS to 16mm film. Many of the programs include teaching materials that are yours to keep after the showing. Company cannot list specific films (though they are classic and popular contemporary movies) because what they offer changes according to their sponsors' current interests.

Ask for: Catalog.

Requirements: Some materials (e.g., the caption film titles) require one of your students have hearing impairment.

NATIONAL EDUCATION GOALS PANEL
1850 M Street, NW, Suite 270
Washington, DC 20036
(202) 632-0952; fax: (202) 632-0957

■ A unique, bipartisan body of state and federal officials created in 1990 to monitor national and state progress toward achieving the eight National Educational Goals. Issues its annual report each September, on the anniversary of the historic Charlottesville Education Summit of 1989. Write to obtain free copies of the 1998 Goals Report and further information about the Panel.

Ask for: Form for free publications.

Requirements: None.

NATIONAL GALLERY TEACHER INSTITUTE
ON MODERN ART
Attn: Julie Springer
Education Division
National Gallery of Art
Washington, DC 20565
(202) 842-6261

■ Because of the crisis facing our schools today, teachers and administrators must work together more closely, supporting one another and taking equal part in framing the curriculum and educating our young. It is this spirit of collaboration and shared learning that underlies the philosophy of the National Gallery of Art National Teacher Institute—a six-day program designed to foster enthusiasm and understanding for art and to make applications to multidisciplinary education.

Prior to 1994, the Institute primarily served teachers. Today, it welcomes teams of principals, administrators, and teachers who are from the same school districts. Principals are invited to apply for this year's program, along with one or two teacher-colleagues. Teachers of all subjects and grade levels are also eligible to apply. Administrators may be, but are not limited to, principals, curriculum specialists, or supervisors. Team applicants should have the general goal of collaboration upon return to school.

Programs typically feature a series of lectures, studio technique demonstrations, hands-on sessions, and tours of the National Gallery's collection of early 20th-century art. Lectures and discussions are led by National Gallery staff as well as outside experts. A visit to the nearby Hirshhorn Museum and Sculpture Garden in Washington provides additional study opportunities.

The Teacher Institute is designed to be a national forum for intellectual renewal for educators by providing information about art and its cultural context and by demonstrating techniques for teaching about art. Unlike school- or university-based programs, the Gallery's Institute offers educators the opportunity to learn through face-to-face encounters with art in a museum setting. The topic of the Institute varies from year to year. Since 1989, more than 800 educators from every state and all U.S. territories have attended.

To receive application materials, educators should send postcards (early in the calendar year) with their name and address to the Education Division at the National Gallery of Art.

The Teacher Institute supplements the National Gallery's extension programs, which serve a national audience through the production and free-loan distribution of instructional materials, including videocassettes, videodiscs, slide programs, and other teaching resources.

Ask for: A new catalog of available materials.

Requirements: Send postcard for program application.

Check Out the Classics

What sort of music can you play for your students after an activity or recess to calm them and shift them back into the classroom learning gear? Well, you'll find a wealth of ideas in *The NPR Guide to Building a Classical CD Collection*, by Ted Libbey (Workman Publishing, 1994, $15.95).

The Classical Child Series, from MetroMusic (see address below) was created to introduce children to classical music by making the arrangements very playful. It is not intended as a replacement for traditional classical music but rather as a fun introduction. The series contains The Classical Child, volumes 1, 2, and 3 and Christmas. For information or copies of the series, check retail stores or call (800) 872-9745.

Equally soothing contemporary music is also available. Adult Contemporary Instrumental Music (often called "New Age") helps students—and teachers(!)—to relax. A variety of companies (listed below) produce these peaceful CDs. While there are currently not any deals in this area (like the Damaged and Defective book program listed earlier), free "samplers" have been marketed in very clever ways.

Music is a beneficial educational tool in three ways: it teaches musical appreciation; it is an excellent way to introduce other cultures; and it can evoke relaxation, calm, and balance. This peaceful music intuitively connects the other all-important themes emphasized in this book: respect for others, for one's self, and for the environment.

Here's a starter list of record companies with which to familiarize yourself. Take this list to a CD store—and enjoy!

ARC MUSIC AMERICA
P.O. Box 2543
Clearwater, FL 34617
(813) 447-3755;
fax: (813) 447-3820

**CANYON RECORDS
PRODUCTIONS**
4143 North 16th Street,
   Suite 6
Phoenix, AZ 85016
(602) 279-5941

DOMO MUSIC INC.
245 South Spalding Drive
Beverly Hills, CA 90212
(310) 557-2100

HEARTS OF SPACE
P.O. 31321
San Francisco, CA 94131
(415) 242-8888

**HIGHER OCTAVE
MUSIC**
23852 PCH, Suite 2C
Malibu, CA 90265
(310) 589-1515
Direct-order line:
   (800) 699-6874

LIVING MUSIC
174 Norfolk Road
P.O. Box 68
Litchfield, CT 06759
(203) 567-8796

METROMUSIC
312 San Francisco Boulevard
San Anselmo, CA 94960
(415) 721-0422;
fax: (415) 721-7232

**NARADA
PRODUCTIONS**
4650 North Port
   Washington Road
Milwaukee, WI 53212-1063
(414) 961-8350

REAL MUSIC
85 Libertyship Way, #207
Sausalito, CA 94965
(415) 331-8273

RYKODISC
27 Congress Street
Salem, MA 01970
(508) 744-7678

**WINDHAM HILL
RECORDS**
8750 Wilshire Boulevard
Beverly Hills, CA 90211-2713
(310) 358-4800;
fax: (310) 358-4802

NEW READERS PRESS

Publishing Division of Laubach Literacy International
Department AS94
P.O. Box 888
Syracuse, NY 13210-0888
(800) 448-8878

■ Your students and perhaps even their parents often struggle because they do not have the basic skills to face the demands of school, work, or life. An excellent resource for helping them is *Adult Basic Education Publishing* from New Readers Press. Call or write this company to learn about their thorough publishing program. Subjects covered include reading, newspaper literacy, pleasure reading, spelling, writing, ESL, Spanish language, math, workplace literacy, family literacy, life skills, social studies, teacher resources, and staff development and training. Titles include *Teaching Adults: A Literacy Resource Book* and *Teacher's Guide: Family Issues, Community Issues, Work Issues.*

Ask for: Catalog.

Requirements: None.

STUTTERING FOUNDATION

(800) 992-9392

■ Offers free and inexpensive information and materials on how to help children who stutter.

Ask for: Free information.

Requirements: None.

TRUSTING KIDS

Attn: Becky Schaller
7719 North Hermitage, G-1
Chicago, IL 60626-1064

■ This free quarterly newsletter helps teachers of five- to eight-year-olds with emotional or behavioral problems. Through the

Children's Music by Jon Anderson

Jon Anderson, best known as the leader of the rock band Yes, has written what could be called a "children's CD": *Angel's Embrace* (Higher Octave Music, 23852 Pacific Coast Highway, Suite 2C, Malibu, CA 90265; (800) 699-6874). Anderson swears that the music, written to be played quietly and "surround" the listener, sends children to sleep; he says that it has even been child tested! Anderson explained that *Angel's Embrace* embodies the ideas he explored in Yes and in duo albums with the Greek composer Vangelis (*Chariots of Fire*). For music of tranquility and healing, there is none better than Jon Anderson.

If you want to learn more about Jon Anderson, you can write to the Opio Foundation, 409 Antoinette Road, Wilmington, NC 28412—this is a newsletter Anderson sells for a nominal fee and then gives the money to UNICEF.

newsletter you can share information, experiences, and questions with others.

Ask for: *Trusting Kids.*

Requirements: State your job title and include first-class postage.

Professional Organizations

Professional organizations offer various benefits, including networking opportunities, conventions, journals and other publications, resources, discounts, voting rights and professional representation, and even credit cards, insurance, health plans, travel advantages, and long-distance calling. Many organizations

Create Your Own Videos to Watch and Loan

Have you ever thought about how your knowledge could be helpful to someone else? In our hi-tech world, it is easy enough to make professional-looking home videos. As an activity, make your own videos of a subject important to your community and distribute them via the school, local library, or video shop. Did you recently give a first-rate lecture? Did your students put together a terrific special report you'd like to share with others? Did your school have a special awareness day on the environment or conflict management that could help others? Tape your work, help your students learn more by teaching others, and start an exchange program with other schools and communities.

have special membership prices for teachers who are still in college, thus providing an inexpensive way to begin affiliation with a professional association. Write these professional organizations for information on how they can be helpful to you.

AMERICAN ALLIANCE FOR HEALTH, PHYSICAL EDUCATION, AND RECREATION (AAHPER)
1201 Sixteenth Street, NW
Washington, DC 20036

AMERICAN ASSOCIATION OF SCHOOL LIBRARIANS (AASL)
50 East Huron Street
Chicago, IL 60611

AMERICAN HOME ECONOMICS ASSOCIATION (AHEA)
2010 Massachusetts Avenue, NW
Washington, DC 20036

AMERICAN INDUSTRIAL ARTS ASSOCIATION (AIAA)
1201 Sixteenth Street, NW
Washington, DC 20036

**ASSOCIATION FOR CHILDHOOD EDUCATION
INTERNATIONAL (ACEI)**
3615 Wisconsin Avenue, NW
Washington, DC 20016

**ASSOCIATION FOR COMPUTERS IN MATHEMATICS
AND SCIENCE TEACHING (ACMST)**
P.O. Box 4455
Austin, TX 78765

**ASSOCIATION FOR EDUCATIONAL
COMMUNICATIONS TECHNOLOGY (AECT)**
1201 Sixteenth Street, NW
Washington, DC 20036

**ASSOCIATION FOR SUPERVISION AND CURRICULUM
DEVELOPMENT (ASCD)**
125 North West Street
Alexandria, VA 22314

COUNCIL FOR LIBRARY RESOURCES, INC. (CLR)
One Dupont Circle
Washington, DC 20036

INTERNATIONAL READING ASSOCIATION (IRA)
800 Barksdale Road
Newark, DE 19714-8139

MUSIC EDUCATORS NATIONAL CONFERENCE (MENC)
1902 Association Drive
Reston, VA 22091

NATIONAL ARTS EDUCATION ASSOCIATION (NAEA)
1916 Association Drive
Reston, VA 22091

NATIONAL ASSOCIATION OF BIOLOGY TEACHERS (NABT)
11250 Roger Bacon Drive
Reston, VA 22090

NATIONAL ASSOCIATION FOR THE EDUCATION OF YOUNG CHILDREN (NAEYC)
1834 Connecticut Avenue, NW
Washington, DC 20009

NATIONAL ASSOCIATION OF GEOLOGY TEACHERS (NAGT)
P.O. Box 368
Lawrence, KS 66044

NATIONAL COUNCIL FOR THE SOCIAL STUDIES (NCSS)
3501 Newark Street, NW
Washington, DC 10016

NATIONAL COUNCIL OF TEACHERS OF ENGLISH (NCTE)
1111 Kenyon Road
Urbana, IL 61801

NATIONAL COUNCIL OF TEACHERS OF MATHEMATICS (NCTM)
1906 Association Drive
Reston, VA 22091

NATIONAL SCIENCE TEACHERS ASSOCIATION (NSTA)
1742 Connecticut Avenue, NW
Washington, DC 20009

PHI DELTA KAPPA (PDK)
Eighth Street and Union Avenue
Bloomington, IN 47401

PHI KAPPA PHI FOUNDATION (PKP)
Box 16000, Louisiana State University
Baton Rouge, LA 70893

Professional Periodicals

The magazines we've listed here offer teaching ideas, tips, projects, and interesting articles to help you help children. They also contain listings of free resources, scholarship ideas, and materials that can assist you in planning your curriculum. With annual subscription prices from $14.95 to $16.95, they're a deal. Call and request a trial issue.

CREATIVE CLASSROOM
P.O. Box 53152
Boulder, CO 80322-3152
(800) 274-1364

INSTRUCTOR
Scholastic Inc.
P.O. Box 53894
Boulder, CO 80321-3894
(800) 544-2917

LEARNING
P.O. Box 54293
Boulder, CO 80322-4293
(800) 753-1843

Conflict Resolution Resources for Teachers and Parents

With the increasing dangers and complications of today's world, what could be more important than implementing a conflict management program to help students and families resolve conflicts peacefully? Conflict resolution has no limits: it can help troubled families learn to communicate, and it can save lives by preventing violence. Start by obtaining appropriate background information.

BREAK THE SILENCE VIDEOTAPE

P.O. Box 514
New York, NY 10013-0514

■ Preventing and addressing child abuse is one of the most important issues you can face as a teacher. (You are legally obligated to report any child abuse to Child Protection Services.) This video, *Break the Silence: Kids Against Child Abuse,* was previously broadcast on network television. It suggests solutions to child abuse, and includes information sheets, statistics, and a message from the National Committee to Prevent Child Abuse.

Ask for: Break the Silence.

Requirements: $7.00 (at-cost price).

CONFLICT RESOLUTION CURRICULUM

Quest International
1984 Coffman Road
P.O. Box 4850
Newark, OH 43058
(800) 446-2700; fax: (614) 522-6580

■ Teach peaceful conflict resolution and how to settle disputes without violence. This kit, which includes curriculum, materials for student and family, posters, workshop information and a video, is particularly important in this age of escalating violence.

Ask for: Conflict resolution kit.

Requirements: Course study for grades 6–8.

Helpful Books

Albert, Linda. *Cooperative Discipline: Classroom Management that Promotes Self-Esteem.* 1989. American Guidance Service, P.O. Box 99, Publishers' Building, Circle Pines, MN.

*Beekman, Susan and Jeanne Holmes. *Battles, Hassles, Tantrums and Tears: Practical Strategies for Coping with Conflict and Making Peace at Home.* 1993. Hearst Books, 1350 Avenue of the Americas, New York, NY 10019.

*Cary, Elizabeth. *Children's Problem Solving Series (Ages 3–8).* 1984. Parenting Press, Inc., P.O. Box 75267, Seattle, WA 98125, (800) 992-6657.

*Cary, Elizabeth. *Kids Can Cooperate.* 1984. Parenting Press, Inc., P.O. Box 75267, Seattle, WA 98125. (800) 992-6657.

Cheatham, Annie. *Annotated Bibliography for Teaching Conflict Resolution in Schools.* 1989. N.A.M.E., 425 Amity Street, Amherst, MA 01002.

Cihak, Mary and Barbara Heron. *Games Children Should Play: Sequential Lessons for Teaching Communication Skills in Grades K–6.* 1980. Scott, Foresman & Co., 1900 East Lake Avenue, Glenview, IL 60025.

Community Board Program, Inc. *Classroom Confliction Resolution Training for Elementary School.* 1987. 1540 Market Street, Room 490, San Francisco, CA 94102.

Community Board Program, Inc. *Confliction Resolution: A Secondary School Curriculum.* 1987. 1540 Market Street, Room 490, San Francisco, CA 94102.

*Dana, Daniel. *Managing Differences.* 1989. MTI International, 22612 West 53rd Terrace, Shawnee, KS 66226.

Drew, Naomi. *Learning the Skills of Peacemaking.* Jalmar Press, 45 Hitching Post Drive, Building 2, Rolling Hills Estates, CA 90274.

Books marked with * are also good for parent education.

Recommended Reading on Thematic Instruction and Brain Research

Armstrong, Thomas. *In Their Own Way*. Los Angeles: Jeremy P. Tarcher, Inc., 1987.

Caine, Geoffrey and Renate Nummela Caine. *Making Connections: Teaching and The Human Brain*. Alexandria, VA: ASCD, 1991.

Gardner, Howard. *Frames of Mind: The Theory of Multiple Intelligences*. New York: Basic Books, 1985.

Gardner, Howard. *The Unschooled Mind: How Children Think and How Schools Should Teach*. New York: Basic Books, 1991.

Kovalik, Susan. *Teachers Make The Difference*. Kent, WA: Susan Kovalik & Associates, 1989.

Kovalik, Susan. *ITI: The Model*. Susan Kovalik & Associates, 1993.

SOURCES FOR ADDITIONAL BOOKS

BOOKS FOR EDUCATORS
P.O. Box 20525
Village of Oak Creek, AZ 86341
(602) 284-2389; fax: (602) 284-0247

INSTRUCTIONAL FAIR, INC.
P.O. Box 1650
Grand Rapids, MI 49501
(800) 253-5469; fax: (800) 543-2690. Free catalog.

INTERACT, LEARNING THROUGH INVOLVEMENT
P.O. Box 997-Y90
Lakeside, CA 92040

ZEPHYR PRESS
3316 North Chapel Avenue
Tucson, AZ 85716-1416
(520) 322-5090; fax: (520) 323-9402

■ Zephyr is a direct mail publisher, therefore their products cannot be found in stores. They will mail orders directly to interested educators. See their catalog for the book *Seven Pathways of Learning* and for conferences on Multiple Intelligences (MI) theory, developed by Howard Gardner of Harvard University's Project Zero.

*Faber, Adele and Elaine Mazlish. *How to Talk So Kids Will Listen and Listen So Kids Will Talk*. 1987. Avon Books, 1350 Avenue of the Americas, New York, NY 10019.

Kriedler, William, *Creative Conflict Resolution: More than 200 Activities for Keeping Peace in the Classroom*. 1980. Scott, Foresman & Co., 1900 East Lake Avenue, Glenview, IL 60025.

Kriedler, William. *Elementary Perspectives 1: Teaching Concepts Peace and Conflict*. 1990. Educators for Social Responsibility, 23 Garden Street, Cambridge, MA 02138.

*Nelson, Jane. *Positive Discipline*. 1987. Ballantine Books, 201 East 50th Street, New York, NY 10022.

*Nelson, Jane and H. Stephen Glenn. *Time Out: Abuses and Effective Uses*. 1991. Sunrise Books, P.O. Box B, Provo, UT 84603, (800) 456-7770.

Schmidt and Friedman. *Creative Conflict Solving for Kids Grades 5–9*. 1983. Grace Abrams Peace Education Foundation, Inc., P.O. Box 19-1153, Miami, FL 33119.

Wichert, Suzzane. *Keeping the Peace: Practicing Cooperation and Conflict Resolution with Preschools*. 1989. New Society Publishers, Santa Cruz, CA 95061.

Creating a Nonviolent Classroom

Teaching conflict resolution in your classroom can help protect you and your students from the escalating violence in today's society. Follow these principles in the classroom.

- Teach and show kids respect.
- Listen to your students.
- Create a stable, firm, yet caring, environment.
- Have clear-cut procedures for all activities—how to stand in line, how to turn in papers, how to work cooperatively.
- Reward positive behavior.
- Establish consequences for behavior.
- Learn conflict resolution in order to defuse potentially violent situations.
- Get the support of your school and the community.
- Know the procedure for action when discipline is needed or when conflict begins.
- Inspire the students. Discuss the ideals of nonviolence and teach its ideals through teaching the lives of history's great nonviolent leaders.
- Teach the "oneness" of the school. It is a haven of respect and unity.

National Educational Research and Development Centers

To improve and strengthen student learning in the United States, the Office of Educational Research and Improvement's (OERI) Office of Research supports 21 university-based National Educational Research and Development Centers. The Research and Development Centers are encouraged by the OERI to ensure that the information (studies, reports, and inexpensive publications) they produce is available to all, makes a difference to teachers, and reaches parents and anyone else who can make meaningful changes in the classroom.

Herein is a list of the 15 Centers we found most applicable to teachers' and parents' education. Write to them for information.

Cultural Diversity and Second Language Learning

NATIONAL CENTER FOR RESEARCH ON CULTURAL DIVERSITY AND SECOND LANGUAGE LEARNING
Attn: Barry McLaughlin, Director
University of California at Santa Cruz
399 Clark Kerr Hall
Santa Cruz, CA 95064
(408) 459-3500; fax: (408) 459-3502

Affiliated Organizations: Center for Applied Linguistics, Linguistic Minority Research Institute of the University of California
OERI Center Monitor: Henrietta Moody, (202) 219-2079

Disadvantaged Students

CENTER FOR RESEARCH ON EFFECTIVE SCHOOLING FOR DISADVANTAGED STUDENTS
Attn: James McPartland, Director
Johns Hopkins University
3505 North Charles Street
Baltimore, MD 21218
(410) 516-0370; fax: (410) 516-6370

Affiliated Organizations: Council of Chief State School Officers; Teachers College, Columbia University; University of California at Santa Barbara; University of Texas at El Paso
OERI Center Monitor: Harold Himmelfarb, (202) 219-2031

Education in the Inner Cities

NATIONAL RESEARCH CENTER ON EDUCATION IN THE INNER CITIES
Attn: Margaret Wang, Director
Temple University
933 Ritter Hall Annex
13th Street and Cecil B. Moore Avenue
Philadelphia, PA 19122
(215) 204-3000; fax: (215) 204-5130

Affiliated Organizations: University of Houston, University of Illinois at Chicago

OERI Center Monitor: Oliver Moles, (202) 219-2211

Evaluation, Standards, and Student Testing

CENTER FOR RESEARCH ON EVALUATION, STANDARDS, AND STUDENT TESTING (CRESST)
Attn: Ronald Dietel, Director of Communications
Graduate School of Education
University of California at Los Angeles
145 Moore Hall
Los Angeles, CA 90024-1522
(310) 206-1532l; fax: (310) 825-3883; E-mail: gopher.cse.ucla; website: www.cse.ucla.edu

Affiliated Organizations: Learning Research Development Center, National Opinion Research Center, RAND Corporation, University of Colorado

OERI Center Monitor: David Sweet, (202) 219-1748

Families, Communities, Schools, and Children's Learning

CENTER ON FAMILIES, COMMUNITIES, SCHOOLS, AND CHILDREN'S LEARNING
Attn: Don Davies and Joyce Epstein, Codirectors
Boston University
605 Commonwealth Avenue
Boston, MA 02215
(617) 353-3309; fax: (617) 353-8444

Affiliated Organizations: Institute for Responsive Education, Johns Hopkins University, University of Illinois at Champaign-Urbana, Wheelock College, Yale University

OERI Center Monitor: Patricia Lines, (202) 219-2223

Gifted and Talented

NATIONAL RESEARCH CENTER ON THE GIFTED AND TALENTED
Attn: Joseph Renzulli, Director
University of Connecticut
362 Fairfield Road U-7
Storrs, CT 06260-2007
(203) 486-4826; fax: (203) 486-2900

Affiliated Organizations: University of Georgia, University of Virginia, Yale University

OERI Center Monitor: Ivor Pritchard, (202) 219-2223

Literature

NATIONAL RESEARCH CENTER ON LITERATURE TEACHING AND LEARNING
Attn: Arthur Applebee, Director
State University of New York at Albany
1400 Washington Avenue
Albany, NY 12222
(518) 442-5026; fax: (518) 442-5933

OERI Center Monitor: Rita Foy, (202) 219-2021

Mathematics

NATIONAL CENTER FOR RESEARCH IN MATHEMATICAL SCIENCES EDUCATION
Attn: Thomas Romberg, Director
University of Wisconsin
1025 West Johnson Street
Madison, WI 53706
(608) 263-3605; fax: (608) 263-3406

Affiliated Organizations: Harvard University, San Diego State University

OERI Center Monitor: Kent Viehoever, (202) 219-2021

Organization and Restructuring of Schools

CENTER ON ORGANIZATION AND RESTRUCTURING OF SCHOOLS

Attn: Thomas Romberg, Director
University of Wisconsin
1025 West Johnson Street
Madison, WI 53706
(608) 263-3605; fax: (608) 263-3406

Affiliated Organizations: Hofstra University, University of Chicago, University of Michigan, University of Minnesota

OERI Center Monitor: Ron Anson, (202) 219-2214

Reading

NATIONAL READING RESEARCH CENTER

Attn: Donna Alvermann and John Guthrie, Codirectors
University of Georgia
318 Aderhold Hall
Athens, GA 30602-7125
(706) 542-3674; fax: (706) 542-3678

Affiliated Organization: University of Maryland at College Park

OERI Center Monitor: Anne P. Sweet, (202) 219-2021

Science

NATIONAL CENTER FOR SCIENCE TEACHING AND LEARNING

Attn: Arthur White and Michael Klapper, Codirectors
Ohio State University
1929 Kenny Road
Columbus, OH 43210-1015
(614) 292-3339; fax: (614) 292-1595

OERI Center Monitor: Wanda Chambers, (202) 219-2021

Student Learning

**NATIONAL RESEARCH CENTER ON
STUDENT LEARNING**
Attn: Robert Glaser, Lauren Resnick, and James Voss,
Codirectors
University of Pittsburgh
3939 O'Hara Street
Pittsburgh, PA 15260
(412) 624-7457; fax: (412) 624-3051

OERI Center Monitor: Judith Segal, (202) 219-2021

Teacher Learning

**NATIONAL CENTER FOR RESEARCH ON
TEACHER LEARNING**
Attn: Robert Floden and Williamson McDiarmid, Codirectors
Michigan State University
116 Erickson Hall
East Lansing, MI 48824-1034
(517) 355-9302; fax: (517) 336-2795

Affiliated Organizations: University of Wisconsin at Madison,
Education Matters, Inc.

OERI Center Monitor: Joyce Murphy, (202) 219-2039

Technology

CENTER FOR TECHNOLOGY IN EDUCATION
Attn: Jan Hawkins, Director
Education Development Center, Inc.
610 West 112th Street
New York, NY 10025
(212) 875-4560; fax: (212) 875-4760

Affiliated Organizations: Bolt, Beranek, & Newman, Inc.;
Brown University; Harvard University

OERI Center Monitor: Ram Singh, (202) 219-2021

Writing

NATIONAL CENTER FOR THE STUDY OF WRITING AND LITERACY

Attn: Sarah Freedman, Director
University of California at Berkeley
5513 Tolman Hall
Berkeley, CA 94720
(510) 643-7022; fax: (510) 643-8479

Affiliated Organization: Carnegie Mellon University

OERI Center Monitor: Stephen Hunt, (202) 219-2253

Other Programs

In addition to the National Research and Development Centers, the Office of Research supports other programs and projects to help improve and strengthen student learning. They include:

FIELD INITIATED STUDIES (FIS)

Supports distinct research projects to advance educational theory and practice. Public and private organizations, agencies, institutions, and individuals compete annually for their awards. Approximately 12 projects are funded each year. For information about application deadlines and abstracts of funded projects, call (202) 219-2223.

STUDIES OF EDUCATION REFORM

Seeks to generate important and useful information that supports future efforts to improve American education at the preschool, elementary, and secondary levels. The program produces technical reports for the research community and practical advice for policymakers and educators. Areas of inquiry are as diverse as early childhood education, student assessment, at-risk students, technology, curriculum reform, and school-to-work transitions. For more information and descriptions of the studies, call (202) 219-2235.

RESEARCH SYNTHESES

Makes the results and findings from Office of Research sponsored activities available in useful forms to teachers, parents, and others interested in knowing more about education trends and issues. For more information and copies of publications, call (202) 219-2079.

Handling a Crisis

Teaching may often feel like a crash course in dealing with crises. But no matter how experienced you are in seeing and coping with the problems of children and their families, we recommend you have emergency numbers on hand and continue to build your basic knowledge of the problems your students may face.

What are the signs of child abuse? Where should you turn when you see them? What are the signs of suicidal behavior? Drug use? What are the deeper problems of the disruptive child (or his or her opposite: the too-well-mannered, over-productive child)? How can you help?

Crisis Coping

In a crisis, it will help to:

- Talk to someone.
- Refer the victim to an agency that can provide help.
- Know where to report a medical, trauma, or assault situation.
- Know the signs of crisis.
- Have emergency numbers and procedures handy.
- Report suspected child abuse to Child Protective Services.
- Dial 911 if you are experiencing any emergency.

Emergency Contacts

Attempts to produce a cohesive National Emergency Hotline have not been heartening. Many crisis centers are poorly funded (or not funded at all) and are therefore dismantled. Few hotlines are national; rather most are regional.

We encourage you to obtain your regional numbers. Call your local County Office of Child Abuse Prevention Council and ask for their resource directory. Here are a few national and regional contacts to get you started:

National Runaway Switchboard (800) 621-4000
The Vanished Children's Alliance (408) 971-4822
National S.T.D. Hotline (800) 227-8922
Cocaine and Drug Abuse Hotline (800) 662-HELP
National AIDS Hotline, Centers for Disease Control
    (800) 342-AIDS
Spanish Language Hotline (800) 344-7432
TDD/Deaf Access (800) 243-7889
The Points of Light Foundation (800) 468-7687

AMERICAN ASSOCIATION FOR WORLD HEALTH
1129 20th Street, NW, Suite 400
Washington, DC 20036-3403
(202) 466-5883

Ask for: Information.

Requirements: None.

THE CAR ACCIDENT FOUNDATION, INC.
Healing Invisible Wounds
203 Washington Street #313
Salem, MA 01970
(978) 744-6784, (888) 351-3340; fax: (978) 744-6789;
E-mail: caraccident@spress.com;
website: http://www.stresspress.com/car

■ Tragically, many students will experience the death of a class-mate sometime in their K–12 years—and the most common cause of death is an automobile accident. A resource to help students come to terms with such loss and begin to heal wounds can begin with a visit to the Car Accident Foundation's website.

The foundation not only gives information for survivors but offers ways a school can order a book or make a donation. A book purchased by the student union or library can be dedicated to the deceased.

Ask for: Information (and remember, the website is free).

Requirements: None.

GENERAL SERVICE OFFICES OF ALCOHOLICS ANONYMOUS (AA)

Grand Central Station
P.O. Box 459
New York, NY 10163
(212) 870-3400; fax: (212) 870-3003

■ AA's sole purpose is to help alcoholics recover through its Twelve Steps program. They do not cover the general subject of alcoholism.

For information on the general subject of alcoholism, we suggest you write the National Council on Alcoholism and Drug Dependence, 12 West 21st Street, 8th Floor, New York, NY 10010, (212) 206-6770. This organization is not affiliated with AA, but it provides a program of public and professional education and community services and is an advocate for the improved treatment of alcoholism. Or, write the National Clearinghouse for Alcohol and Drug Information (address listed later in this section).

For information about Al-Anon, organization for the family and friends of the alcoholic, contact Al-Anon Family Group Headquarters, Inc., P.O. Box 862, Midtown Station, New York, NY 10018-0862, (212) 302-7240.

Ask for: Information.

Requirements: None.

NATIONAL ASSOCIATION OF ANOREXIA NERVOSA AND ASSOCIATED DISORDERS (ANAD)

Box 7
Highland Park, IL 60035
(708) 831-3438

Ask for: Information.

Requirements: None.

NATIONAL CLEARINGHOUSE FOR ALCOHOL AND DRUG INFORMATION (NCADI)

U.S. Department of Health and Human Services
Public Health Service
Alcohol, Drug Abuse, and Mental Health Administration
P.O. Box 2345
Rockville, MD 20852
(301) 468-2600 or (800) 729-6686

■ NCADI can meet your alcohol and other drug problem prevention and treatment needs. Ask about videos, free materials, brochures, posters, reports, literature searches, referral information, and much, much more . . .

Ask for: Whatever information you need.

Requirements: None.

NATIONAL COALITION AGAINST DOMESTIC VIOLENCE

P.O. Box 18749
Denver, CO 80218-0749
(303) 839-1852

Ask for: Information.

Requirements: None.

NATIONAL SELF-HELP CLEARINGHOUSE
Graduate School and University Center of CUNY
25 West 43rd Street, Suite 620
New York, NY 10036-7406
(212) 354-8525

Ask for: General information.

Requirements: None.

RACISM AND BIGOTRY ANONYMOUS (RABA)
256 Farallones
San Francisco, CA 94112-2939
(415) 587-4207 or (800) 587-4207

Ask for: Information.

Requirements: None.

SPECIAL PRODUCTS
Dept. RG
34 Romeyn Avenue
Amsterdam, NY 12010
(518) 843-2162

■ Excellent value resource to pass along to parents.

Ask for:
- Kinderprint child identification. Parents should have one for each child. Self-inking strips allow you to fingerprint children for permanent record. Also includes safety tips and recommends other information on children that should be recorded.
- The Sitter. This magnet-backed note board is ideal to keep on the refrigerator for easy access by your baby-sitter. Feel at ease knowing your sitter can quickly find emergency numbers and other important information.

Requirements: $1.00 and SASE per each.

STUDENTS AGAINST DRUNK DRIVING (SADD)

P.O. Box 800
Marlboro, MA 01752
(508) 481-3568

■ Mission is "to provide students with the best prevention and intervention tools to deal with issues of underage drinking, impaired driving, drug abuse, and other destructive decisions and their consequences." SADD offers a solid packet of information (including A Contract for Life Between Parent and Teenager) on the complex issue of drugs and youth.

Ask for: Information packet.

Requirements: None.

Locate Your Local . . .

- battered women's shelter
- Child Abuse and Family Violence Prevention Council
- crisis line
- suicide intervention hotline
- grief counseling service
- rape crisis center
- survivors of incest support group
- Planned Parenthood office
- Parents Without Partners chapter
- kids talk-line
- child care center
- Red Cross chapter
- food (emergency) distribution center
- housing agency
- agency on aging (senior information)
- elder abuse prevention program
- Alzheimer's disease and related disorders organization
- United Way office
- Smokers Anonymous group

- American Cancer Society chapter
- American Lung Association chapter
- National Cancer Institute chapter
- American Heart Association chapter
- Narcotics Anonymous chapter
- Poison Control Center
- psychiatric emergency provider

Chapter Eleven

Community Involvement with the Classroom

Throughout this book, you have seen examples of corporations, the government, and the community offering unbelievably good deals for teachers. We hope it was a pleasant discovery. But the "living" network behind this book—the idea that all of us can help fill the resource gaps and thus contribute to the helping profession of teaching—doesn't stop when you shut this book. That is, not unless you stop. You must take these ideas and extend them further and further. Teachers must tap communities, corporations, and everyday people to help fill needs for special projects and everyday classroom needs.

Interact.

Get involved.

Get others involved.

Try sending a letter home to parents to help find what resources you already have in your classroom. Are your students' parents engineers? Recycling experts? Clerks in a fabric store? Ask them to contribute not just materials but themselves to any number of school projects—school clean-ups, field trips, or science experiments, to name a few.

Go into the community! Almost every large corporation wants to improve public relations, and whom better to help than you, the public servant? Companies have budgets built to give money to schools, and indeed they get tax write-offs for doing just that.

Call your local corporation and ask to speak to someone in corporate relations. Ask what they might offer you in terms of support or materials. Or ask them to underwrite a field trip. Ask your local Safeway for a bread or bakery donation for an Open House. Ask parents and grandparents to help wash cars on Saturday. Get carpet samples from a carpet dealer to make a warm reading section in your classroom. Ask the local nursery for plants to spruce up your room. Make a list. Tell local businesses you're trying to make your classroom a safe, comforting environment.

Give the community the opportunity to contribute. Sometimes people want to help and just don't know how. Others will contribute because they feel they are helping in the educational process. The more your community is involved—whether you teach in the inner-city or rural America—the more your school is a center for the community, and the safer and better off your school and the community is going to be.

Interactive involvement is all about giving and getting back so we can give more to the unbelievably good cause of teaching kids.

Corporate Community Service

Increasingly, corporate America is getting involved with nonprofit organizations and the government to help find real solutions to social problems. Many corporate community service programs make a difference. For further information, contact: The Points of Light Foundation, 1737 H Street, NW, Washington, DC 20006, (202) 223-9186.

The Donations Industry

Companies are turning excess inventory and equipment into a corporate advantage for both their business and for schools.

Why?

By donating, these companies can claim nonprofit, tax-exempt status (IRS 501(c)(3)). They help the schools while they get a corporate advantage in the form of:

- tax write-offs
- expedited tax documentation
- savings on shipping costs
- restored warehouse space
- distribution of product overruns
- scholarships awarded in the corporation's name

For information on this virtually untapped and tremendous resource, contact:

EDUCATIONAL ASSISTANCE LIMITED
P.O. Box 3021
Glen Ellyn, IL 60138
(708) 690-0010; fax: (708) 609-0565

■ This company operates College Opportunity Programs.

GIFTS IN KIND INTERNATIONAL
333 North Fairfax Street
Alexandria, VA 22314
(703) 836-2121; fax: (703) 549-1481

NATIONAL ASSOCIATION FOR THE EXCHANGE OF INDUSTRIAL RESOURCES (NAEIR)
560 McClure Street
Galesburg, IL 61401
(800) 562-0955

 **Bridges Project**

Debbie Sullivan of Lafayette School in Oakland, California, developed an idea on how to "bridge the gap" of economic and racial borders. She began a project that would involve her urban school, a suburban school, and a rural school. The three schools interacted by becoming pen pals and even visited each other at least two times during the year. They even shared resources: the rural school had a bus that they let the other schools use and the suburban school provided parent drivers. The project turned out to be an excellent melding of community and resources. The schools took field trips together and worked on projects together. One such project was to come up with ideas on what to do to convert a military base (San Francisco's Treasure Island) after the base was closed. As a culminating activity all three schools visited Treasure Island. The experience helped to defuse stereotypes the students had about kids from the other areas.

Other Places to Fish for Donations

Write to computer companies and other corporations to see where they distribute their old systems when they upgrade to new computers. Be sure to ask if they provide some business-education partnership work so you have help teaching the system, and some software you and your students understand.

Befriend your local grocery store manager(s). See if they are interested in offering you reduced or free food and materials, e.g., loaves of day-old bread for your back-to-school night, open house, or fund-raiser day. (Bread can be used to make sandwiches to sell, or to feed hungry volunteers.) You may have to offer something in return—a PR blurb in a school program or a mention in the community paper—but you will probably discover you have some good-hearted neighbors in your town (or just folks who see a sensible way to dispose of a perishable product).

Check out garage sales (and friends who are redecorating) to see if you can obtain things to warm up your classroom (e.g., couches, carpet, plants, chairs).

Ask your local carpet dealership or nursery for a bona fide donation for a good cause: your classroom. Do the same for school supplies in drug stores and office supply stores. (Offer a thank-you letter on school stationery, and the store will get a write-off on its taxes.)

Speak with your area's major sports franchise's community relations department. They may help sponsor an event such as a carnival, a wine tasting for adults, a raffle, or a basketball contest featuring teachers vs. local retired pro football heroes.

You might also ask them for donations. Perhaps you could sponsor a function where a famous sports figure attends (to attempt *that*, contact the franchise's community relations department). That way you can sell tickets to your dinner, raffle, wine tasting, or sports day advertising "Featuring Socializing Hour with a member of the . . . ." More likely, the community relations director will send a generous sampling of team PR materials for a raffle (signed pictures of players, an autographed football to auction, seats to a game, etc.).

The National Football League (NFL) has an incredible variety of programs in which they interact with the community. Programs include:

- The NFL salute to educators nationwide via American Education Week.
- Many educational projects in each local area.
- The NFL Teacher of the Month Award.
- The NFL FACT Program (Football and Academics: A Championship Team) which uses NFL trading cards as a learning tool in selected 4th-grade classrooms in all the NFL cities.

A Tennis Program to Inspire Ideas of Your Own

With the help of your local United States Tennis Association (USTA), you can start your own Juniors Tennis Program. Take a tip from Debbie Sullivan from Oakland, California, and organize a school donation project. Debbie called CES Index, a company for which she had previously worked, and was able to gain support to provide a juniors' tennis program. She explained to them that hers was a school in need, and the company replied generously. She was able to equip her thirty-three 5th and 6th graders with tennis racquets, T-shirts, and after-school tennis skills workshops. Also, she was able to rally enough support to have an assembly with tennis star Monica Montoya as a special guest. As a culminating activity the company threw the school a tennis carnival, got Ben and Jerry's to donate twenty-foot-long ice cream sundaes, and got Wilson to donate tennis hats for the kids.

NFL
410 Park Avenue
New York, NY 10022
(212) 758-1500; fax: (212) 826-3454

Human Resources

Everyone has something he or she can contribute to your classroom, whether it is as a speaker, helper, or worker. Consider these possibilities.

- Every parent's job or hobby could be of interest.
- Someone may have particular skills that could be useful to your class.

- Friends, relatives, coworkers, and neighbors could tell stories, help with projects, and donate time or materials.
- Grandparents and aunts and uncles could come and discuss a personal story or viewpoint about a historical situation that the class is studying.
- Scan your community and see who can offer an interesting talk or hands-on experience. Remember, most people enjoy talking about their work. Invite firefighters, police officers, butchers, bakers, immigrants, artists, authors, musicians, and business-persons, so your students are exposed to different points of view.

Interactive Involvement

Interactive involvement is simply two-way communication resulting in an action for a mutually beneficial experience. Use this book's ideas, addresses, and the letter forms in this chapter (all of which may be photocopied) to reach out.

Stay involved and help others get involved.

Write Us with Suggestions, Comments, and Questions

———————
Date

———————————————
Your Name

———————————————
School

———————————————
Address

———————————————
City, State, Zip

Unbelievably Good Deals That You Absolutely Can't Get
   Unless You're a Teacher
Box 6597
Moraga, CA 94570 USA
relayer@ccnet.com

———————————————————————————

———————————————————————————

———————————————————————————

———————————————————————————

———————————————————————————

———————————————————————————

———————————————————————————

———————————————————————————

Sincerely,

For Companies Interested in Being Included

Date

*Unbelievably Good Deals That You Absolutely Can't Get
   Unless You're a Teacher*
Box 6597
Moraga, CA 94570 USA
Email: relayer@ccnet.com

Our business is interested in being listed in the next edition of *Unbelievably Good Deals That You Absolutely Can't Get Unless You're a Teacher*. We've filled out the form below to tell you about ourselves.

Address and number to be listed

Information on the product/service provided

Whom to write or call to obtain product/service

What requirements are needed to apply (if any)

When to apply

Any restrictions

Specific item(s) teachers should request

Sincerely,

Index